THE TRAIL OF
PAINTED PONIES

THE TRAIL OF PAINTED PONIES INC.™

SCOTTSDALE • ARIZONA

Cover Art: La Marr, Maria Ryan, Kevin Kilhoffer
Cover Photography: Bryn Wilkins
Cover Design: Karlynn Keyes, Bryn Wilkins

This book was conceived and produced by:
The Trail of Painted Ponies, Inc.
P.O. Box 2629
Carefree, AZ 85377-2629
Phone: 480-459-5700   Fax: 480-361-5342

Visit our website at: www.trailofpaintedponies.com

Layout and Design:
Karlynn Keyes, Rod Barker, Bryn Wilkins, Evelio Mattos, and Jean-Louis Husson

ISBN-13: 978-0-9760319-2-5
ISBN-10: 0-9760319-2-2

Library of Congress Cataloguing-in Publication Data available

Printed in China

Contents

Crystal
Olena Kalayda

Pony Expressionism

Not long ago an article appeared in the Arts section of The New York Times that examined the state of contemporary sculpture in this country. The conclusion was, "We are in a lull and no artist is making very large or deep changes in our sense of what sculpture can or should be. But who knows. Any day now the next big thing could hit, opening up a brave, new, three-dimensional world."

We think that world is already here, in the form of the extraordinary artwork that has been generated by The Trail of Painted Ponies. We think that by inviting the best artists of our time to let their imaginations run wild on the three-dimensional canvas of a horse, that we have introduced something new, exciting and exceptional into the contemporary art scene. Something that has never been seen before. Something that is nothing less than a new American art movement... one that deserves a name of its own, and that we call "Pony Expressionism."

The medium for our artwork is a national icon. No animal is identified as closely with our history, our national character, our dreams, as the horse. As a symbol of beauty, strength and freedom, the horse has no equal. The fertility and versatility of this medium, that is celebrated with every Painted Pony, is not only entertaining and enriching, but has broadened our perception of Art itself.

It is our humble belief that our inspired pairing of sculpture and painting is giving artists an unprecedented opportunity to explore an artistic road less traveled; that it is producing a dazzling collection of work that challenges the boundaries of tradition; and that in fact is opening up that "brave, new three-dimensional world."

Rod Barker

President/Executive Director

Artists at Work

To witness the artistic process deepens our appreciation of the skill involved in going from inspiration to creation. In recognition of the First Americans who painted and dressed their horses with an aesthetic sensibility, spiritual depth and expressive power that deserves a place among the world's great artistic traditions, *The Trail of Painted Ponies* partnered with *Southwest Art* magazine on the national competition, "The Native Art of Horse Painting." As well as producing an historic collection of original artwork, it also generated a photo album of artists with their Ponies-in-Progress.

Sunkan-Wakan & Dreamwalker
Ben Wright

Prairie Horizon
Bob Coonts

Sacred Paint
Gary Montgomery

Navajo Black Beauty
Barbara Duzan

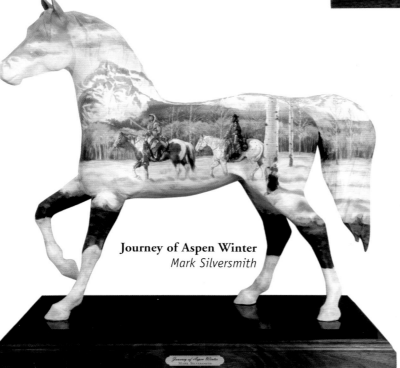

Journey of Aspen Winter
Mark Silversmith

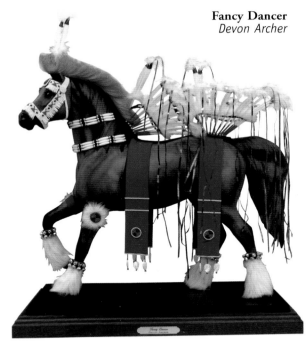

Fancy Dancer
Devon Archer

Storyteller-The Legend of the Dance
Kay Payne

Sounds of Thunder
Bill & Traci Rabbit

Copper Enchantment
Lynn Bean

Native Jewel Pony
Maria Ryan

Rolling Thunder
Aloma Wolfington

Lost Chiefs
Ritch Gaiti

Kindred Spirits
Debbie Hughbanks

Dream Warriors
Ross Lampshire

Spirits of the Northwest
Laurie Holman

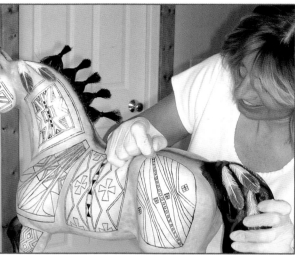

Cheyenne Painted Rawhide
Liz Chappie-Zoller

Salmon-Crow Pony
Priscilla Patey

Indian Pony Life Story
Denise Brown

Wie-Tou
Barbara Janowitz

Runs the Bitteroot
Kevin Kilhoffer

Homage to the Masters

Inspiration comes from many sources. Imagining what the Masters might have created had they been given the opportunity to paint a Pony prompted artwork that evoked the style, technique and imagery of Hokusai, Degas, Van Gogh, Dali, and O'Keeffe.

Hokusai's Great Wave
Mary Sweet

Go Van Gogh
Star Liana York

Homage to Degas
Julian Robles

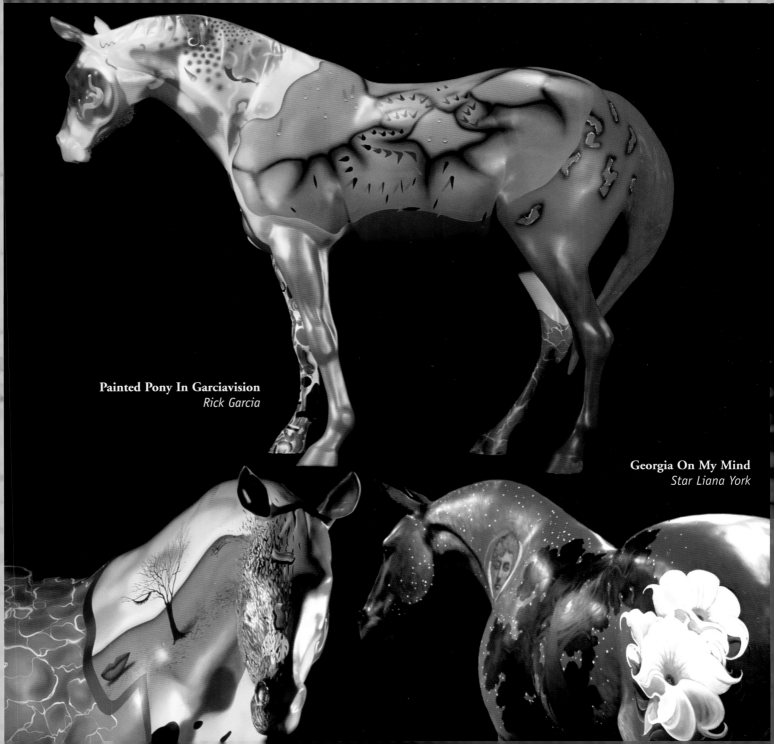

Painted Pony In Garciavision
Rick Garcia

Georgia On My Mind
Star Liana York

O'Keeffe Country
Star Liana York

Native American Ponies

There was a time when Indian art was neglected and overlooked, but not today, and not with The Trail of Painted Ponies. In recognition of the exciting and innovative contemporary Indian art that is being produced, a special effort was made to attract the most talented Native artists in America.

Artists from more than thirty different tribes welcomed the opportunity, producing a beautiful and authentic collection of artwork that carries on centuries of tradition, reveals the different cultures and societies that make up Native America, and expresses the uniquely individual touch of each artist.

The Magician
Anderson Kee, Navajo

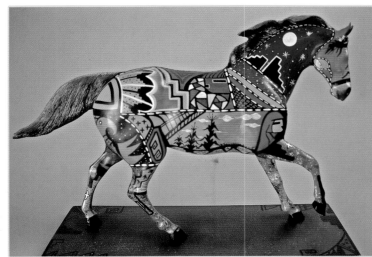

Ghost Horse
Bill Miller, Mohican

Grandfather's Journey
Buddy Tubinaghtewa, Hopi

War Pony
Rance Hood, Comanche

Caballito-Scape Con Estrellitas
Amado Pena, Yacqui

I Stand For My Horse
Beverly Blacksheep, Navajo

Crow War Pony
Kevin Red Star, Crow

Tse-Weeh-Gia-Queejo
Margarete Bagshaw-Tindel, Santa Clara Pueblo

The Swiftness of an Eagle and the Strength of a Bear
Art Menchego, Santa Ana Pueblo

Apache
Warren Sago, Apache

Butterfly Horse
Gregory Lomayesva, Hopi

Horse of the Rising Sun
George Toya, Jemez

Many Horses
Michael Horse, Zuni

Night Flight
Ed Noisecat, Salish

Pueblo Pony
Arlo Namingha, Hopi

Tlingit Robed Horse
Clarissa Hudson, Tlingit

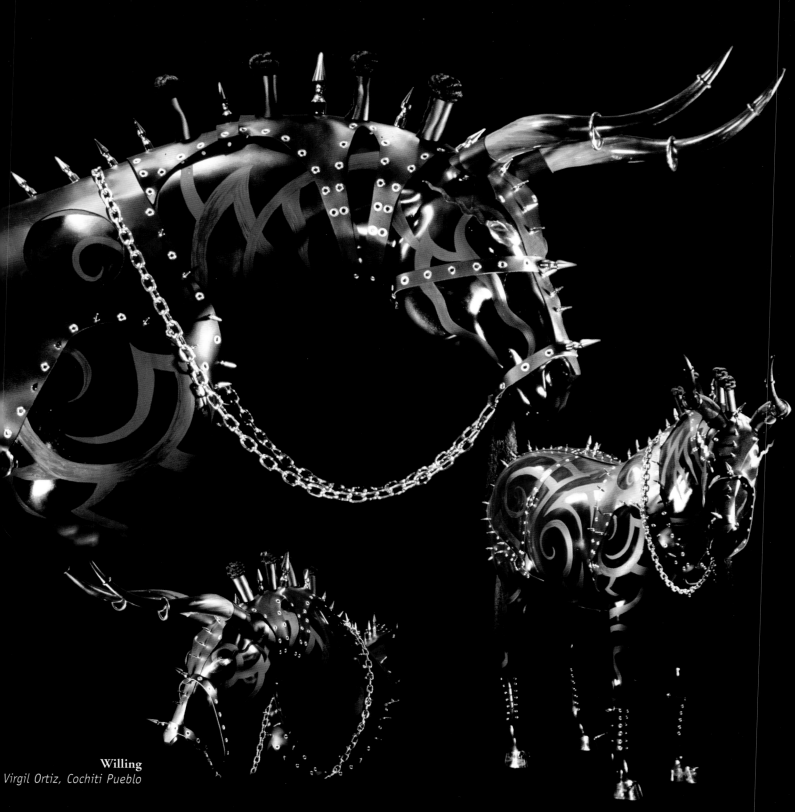

Willing
Virgil Ortiz, Cochiti Pueblo

Love as Strong as a Horse
Jesse Hummingbird, Cherokee

Tewa Pony
Tom Tapia, Tesuque Pueblo

Mad Cow Pony
Bernie Granados, Apache

Horse From The Four Directions
David K. John, Navajo

Lowrider
Ramona Sakiestewa, Hopi

Blue Medicine
Mary Iron Eyes, Osage

When They Ran With Freedom
Benjamin Nelson, Navajo

Indian Summer
Buddy Tubinaghtewa, Hopi

Lightning Bolt Colt
Dyanne Strongbow, Choctaw

Dream Horses

Around the world, horses have appeared in myths as mystical representations of beauty and freedom. In the diverse hands of Painted Pony artists, they were portrayed as magical creatures capable of kicking up their heels and galloping freely across fields of dreams and fantasy.

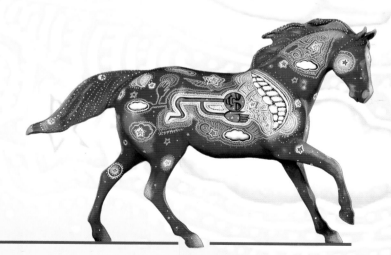

I Dreamed I Was A Blue Horse
Joel Nakamura

Renewal of Life
Natasha Isenhour

Kiri Tuhi (Skin Art)
Joe Clarke & Jamie Schene

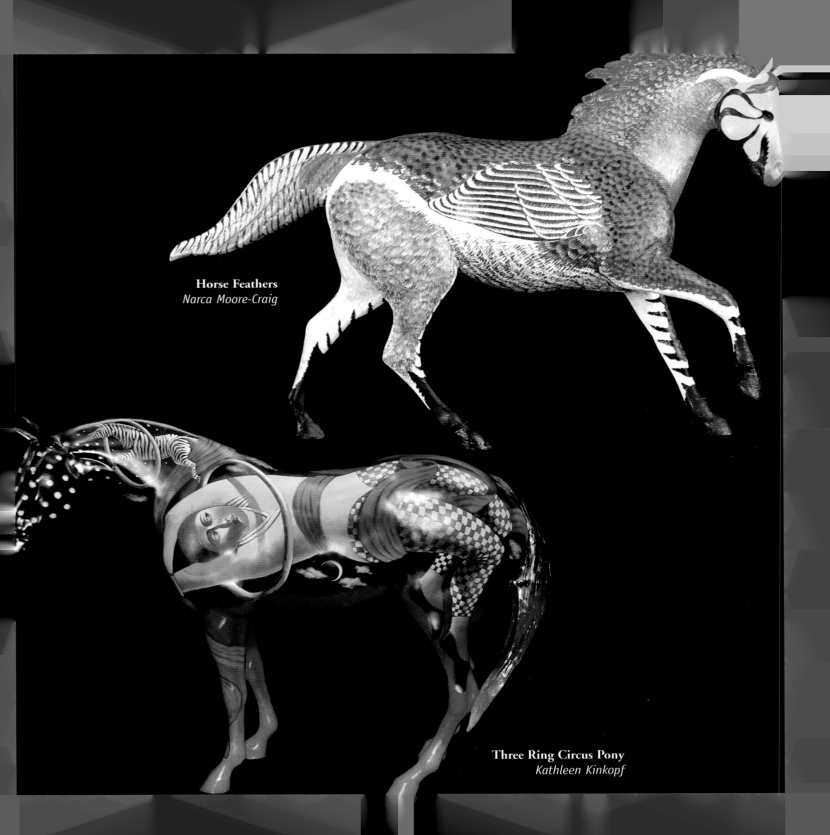

Horse Feathers
Narca Moore-Craig

Three Ring Circus Pony
Kathleen Kinkopf

It's All Greek To Me
Tavlos

End of the Rainbow
Dorothea Von Eckhardt

Dream Horse
Janee Hughes

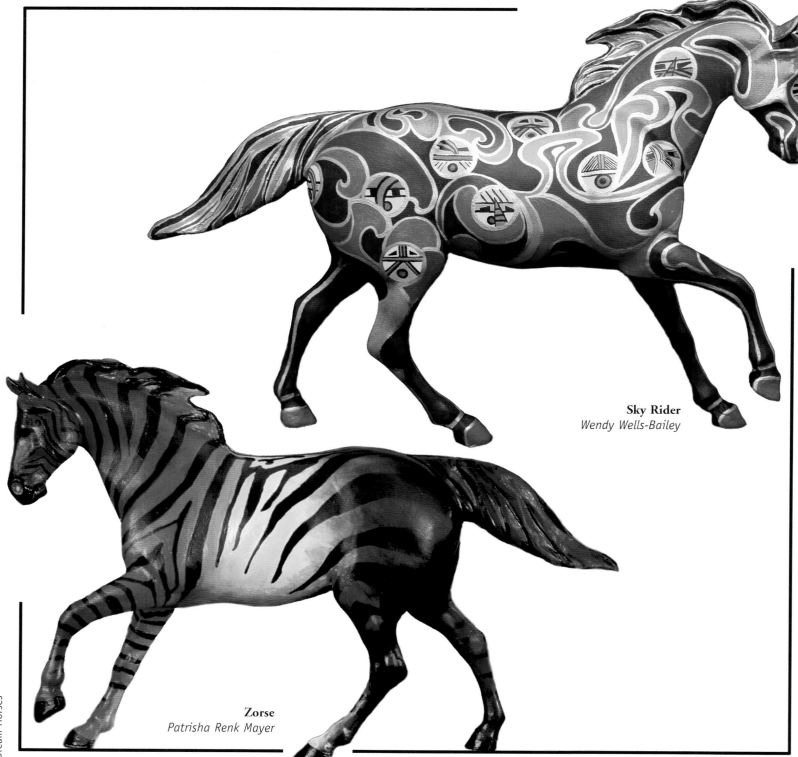

Sky Rider
Wendy Wells-Bailey

Zorse
Patrisha Renk Mayer

Silver Lining
Star Liana York

Heavenly Pony
Noel Espinoza

Sky of Enchantment
Ilsa Magener

Music Horses

From the equestrian ballets of the 17th century, when costumed horses performed intricately choreographed figures to music, to the circular parades of carousel horses whirling to the rollicking tunes of an organ, horses and music have had a colorful relationship that struck a chord in many Painted Pony artists.

Singing Cowboy Pony
Gene Dieckhoner

Jazz on a Hot Tin Roof
Kim Wiggins

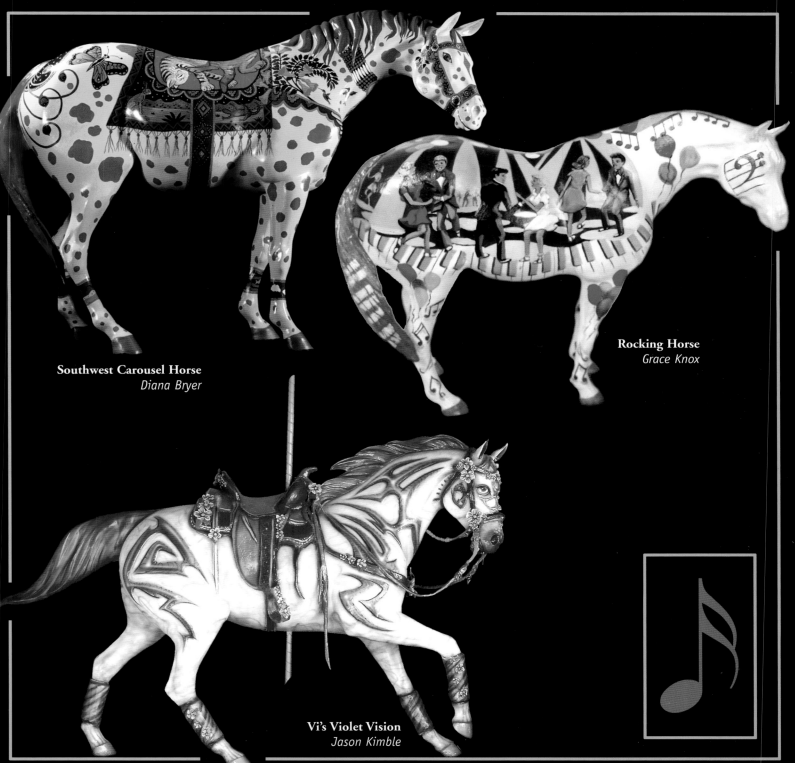

Southwest Carousel Horse
Diana Bryer

Rocking Horse
Grace Knox

Vi's Violet Vision
Jason Kimble

Kokopelli Pony
Joel Nakamura

Young at Heart Horses

For little boys it is the excitement and drama represented by knights jousting on horseback and cowboys herding cattle; for little girls it is the pageantry of horse parades and freedom of pleasure riding. The delight is the same. Horses transport youth to another world, as do those Ponies painted with a youthful spirit.

Children's Prayer Pony
The Youth of America

Dog and Pony Show
Letticia Garcia

Children of the Garden
Connie Garcia

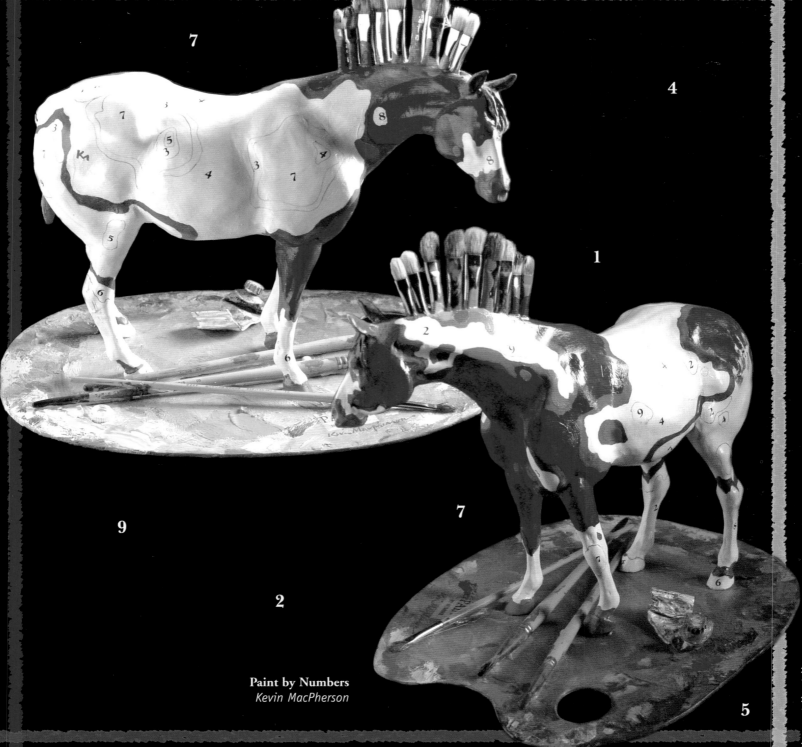

Paint by Numbers
Kevin MacPherson

Snowflake
Judith Fudenski

Nutcracker Pony
Janee Hughes

Lady Ledoux
Inger Jirby

Kitty Cat's Ball
Elizabeth Lewis-Scott

Russian Folk Tale Pony
Bonny

Animal Kingdom

The horse has always occupied a special place in the hierarchy of the animal kingdom. For many artists its stature is so exalted that it is capable of comfortably carrying the entire animal kingdom on its back.

Wilderness Roundup
Mitzi Bower

CowPony
Lori Musil

Take A Walk On The Wild Side
Gene Dieckhoner

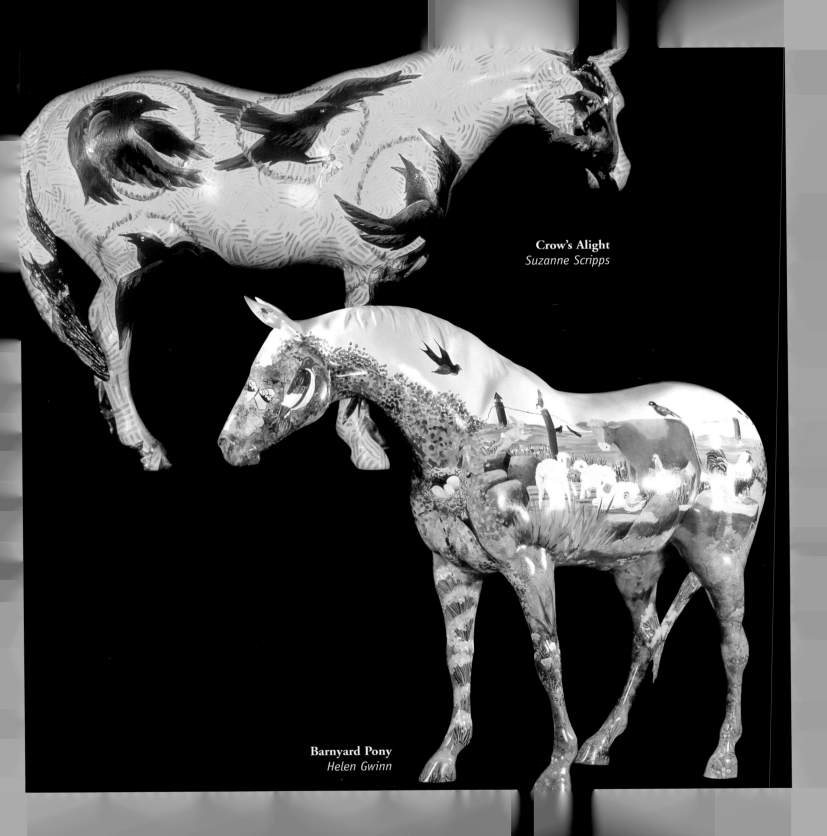

Crow's Alight
Suzanne Scripps

Barnyard Pony
Helen Gwinn

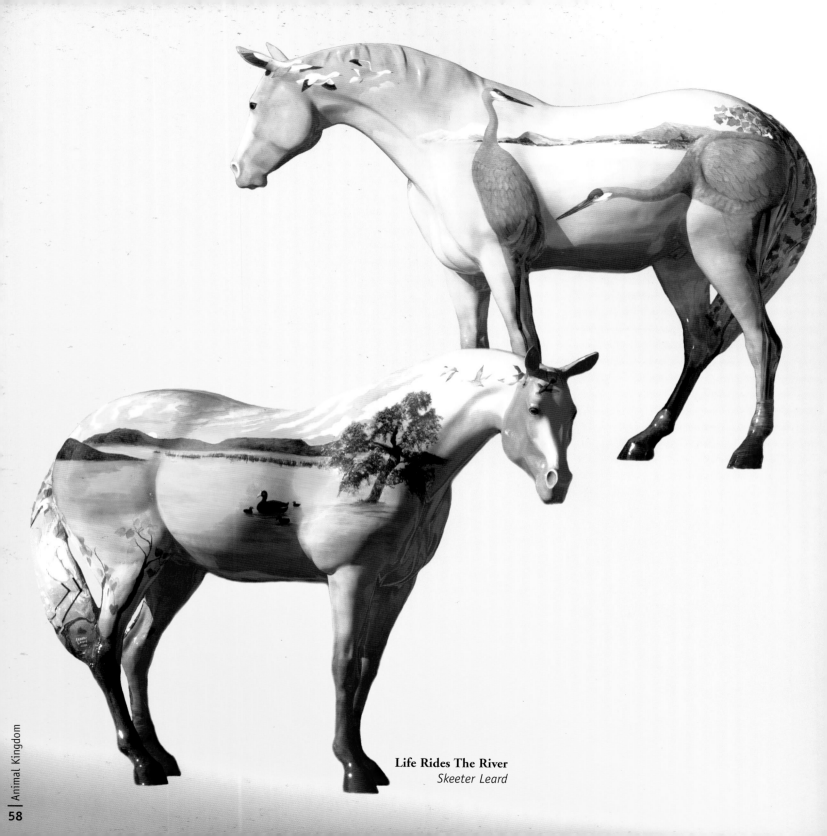

Life Rides The River
Skeeter Leard

Year of the Horse
Lori Musil

Incognito
Janee Hughes

Sea Horses

Seahorses come in an amazing variety of sizes and shapes. Thirty-five species of the ocean variety occur worldwide, and they have the ability to instantly change color, camouflaging themselves as seaweed or coral.

As for the land variety, five Ponies were painted along the seahorse theme, and they too display a chameleon-like quality. Each magically captures a different aquatic look.

Sea Horse
Grace Knox

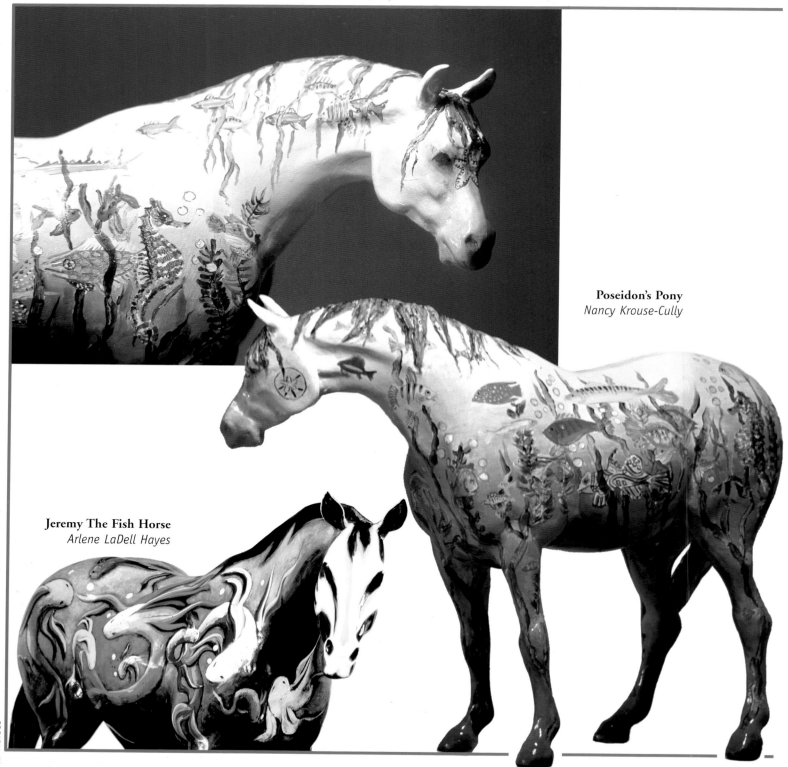

Poseidon's Pony
Nancy Krouse-Cully

Jeremy The Fish Horse
Arlene LaDell Hayes

Tropical Reef Horse
Laurie Holman

Fishback Rider
Patrick Coffaro

Spanish Horses

The horse, hunted into extinction, was reintroduced to North America in the Sixteenth Century when Spanish Conquistadors began to arrive with domesticated horses in the holds of their ships. A horse culture spread rapidly across the New World, creating a legacy that would be remembered proudly by artists of Spanish descent.

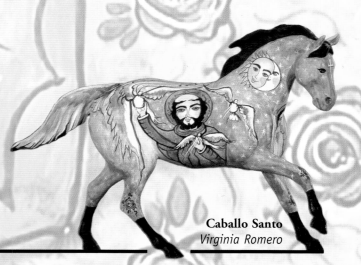

Caballo Santo
Virginia Romero

Sacred Heart
Ed Sandoval

Caballo Brillante
Roger Montoya

Maize Mustang
Pola Lopez

Milagro Pony
Connie Garcia

Sabanilla Bella
Frederico Vigil

Mesoqua Pony
Manuel Salas

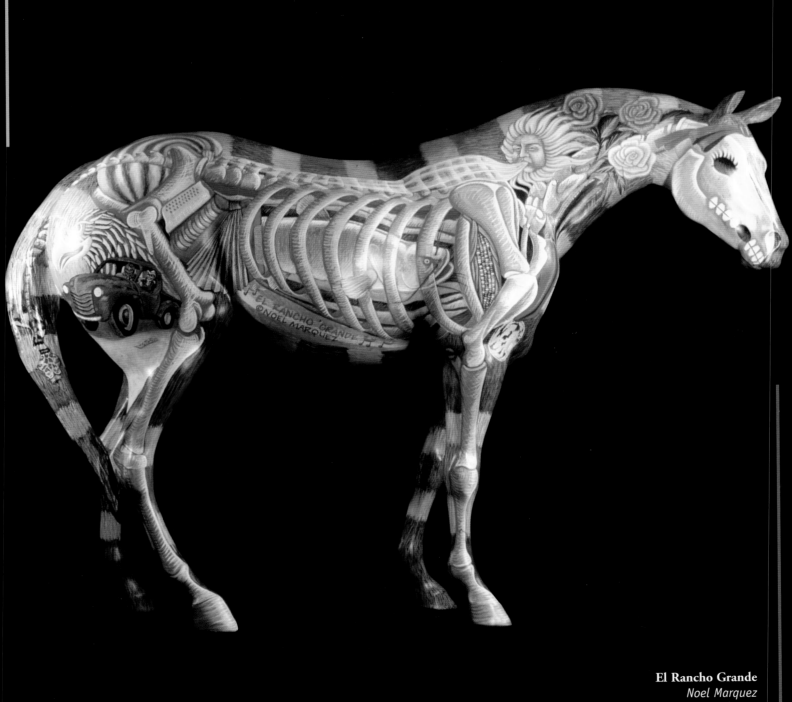

El Rancho Grande
Noel Marquez

1910
Noel Espinoza

Landscape Ponies

It was on horseback that man first traveled across the vast and beautiful American landscape. Historically, artists have shown horses as an integral feature of landscape scenes. It was a logical extension for Painted Pony artists to see the horse itself as a canvas for rendering landscapes.

Lighthorse
Lynn Vanlandingham

Your Everyday Garden Variety
Michael Campbell

Pony Tails
Fran Larsen

Night Peony
Marianne Hornbuckle

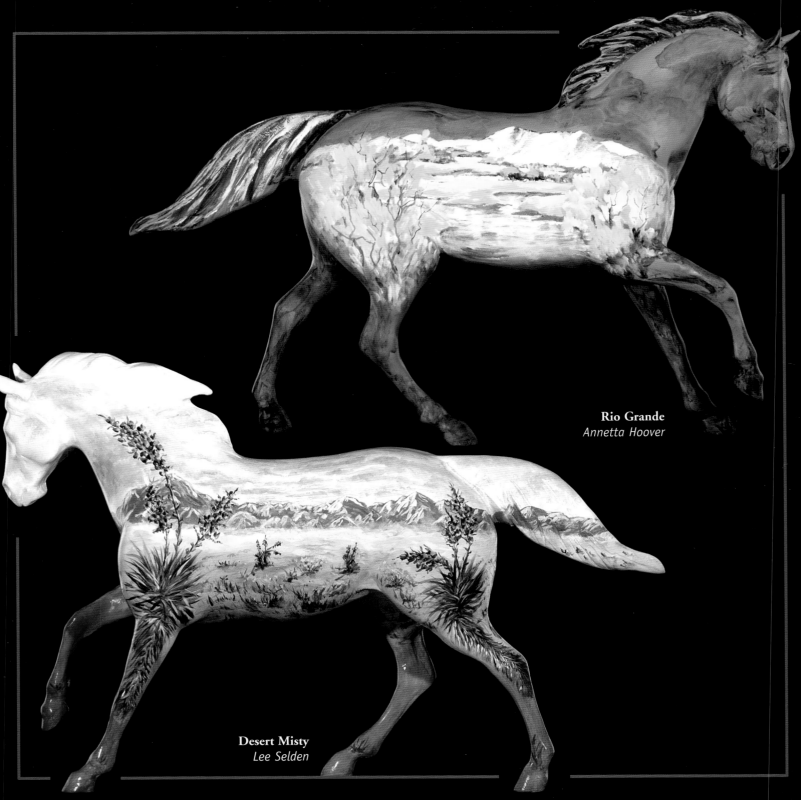

Rio Grande
Annetta Hoover

Desert Misty
Lee Selden

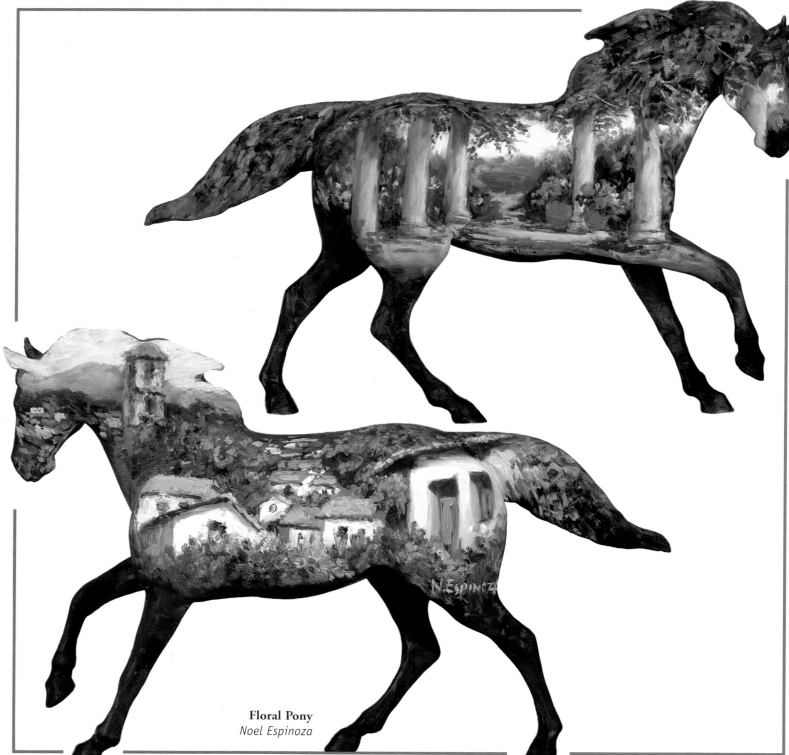

Floral Pony
Noel Espinoza

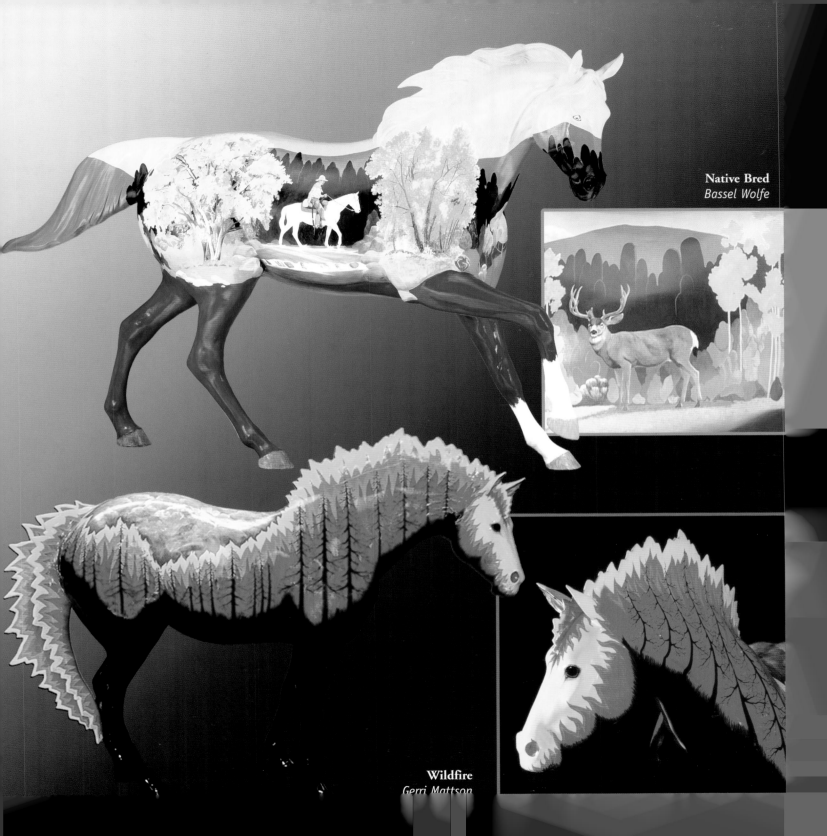

Native Bred
Bassel Wolfe

Wildfire
Gerri Mattson

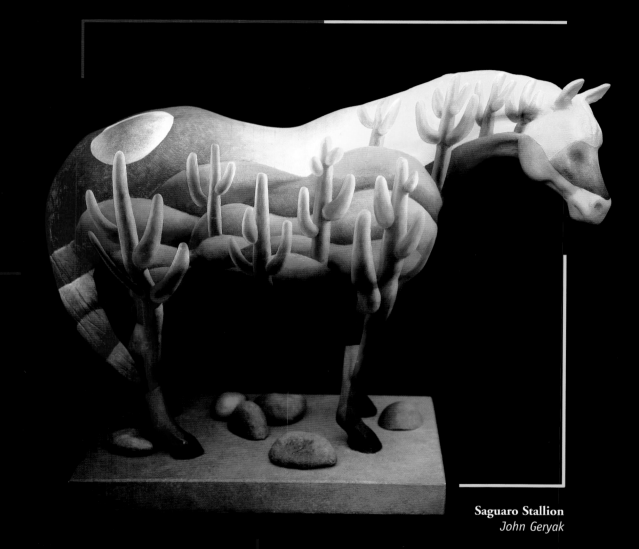

Saguaro Stallion
John Geryak

Southwestern Horses

Nostalgia for the New World conquerors, the Native Americans who became "the Lord of the Plains" once they learned to ride, the mountain men who came down from the Rocky Mountains and the cowboys who drove herds of cattle across these lands, continues to inspire many contemporary American artists.

Unity
Georges Monfils

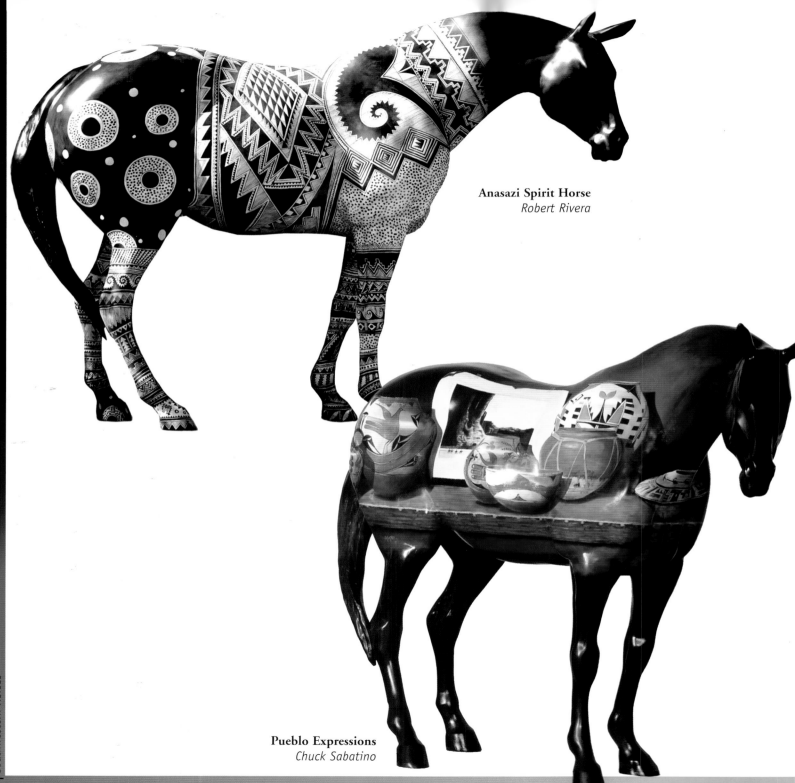

Anasazi Spirit Horse
Robert Rivera

Pueblo Expressions
Chuck Sabatino

Spirit War Pony
Tavlos

Ceremonial War Horse
Carole LaRoche

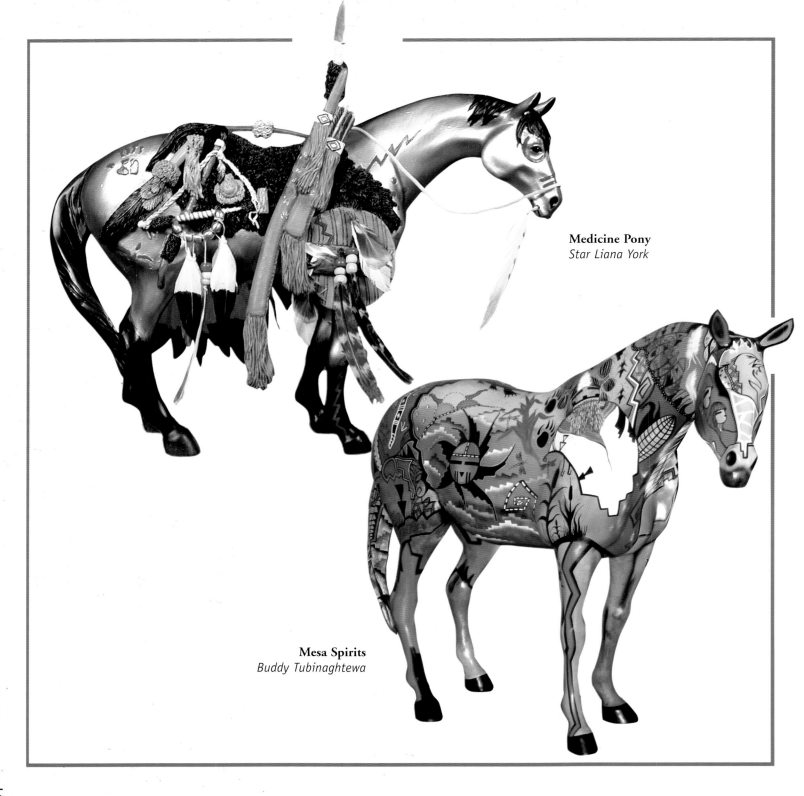

Medicine Pony
Star Liana York

Mesa Spirits
Buddy Tubinaghtewa

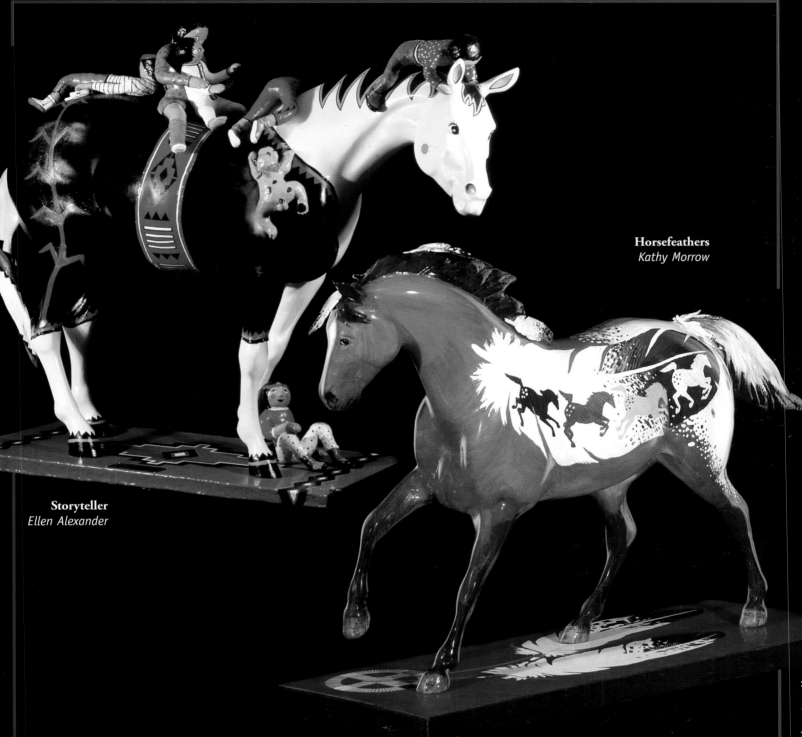

Horsefeathers
Kathy Morrow

Storyteller
Ellen Alexander

Fetish Pony
Lynn Bean

Patriotic Ponies

As a symbol of strength and freedom, the horse is an American icon. From the historic ride of Paul Revere to the triumphs of the American Cavalry to the riderless horse that led President John F. Kennedy's funeral procession, the horse has occupied a special place in our history, and proudly represented the national spirit.

Give Me Wings
Kathy Morrow

Quarter Horse
Kathy Morawski

Yankee Doodle
Grace Knox

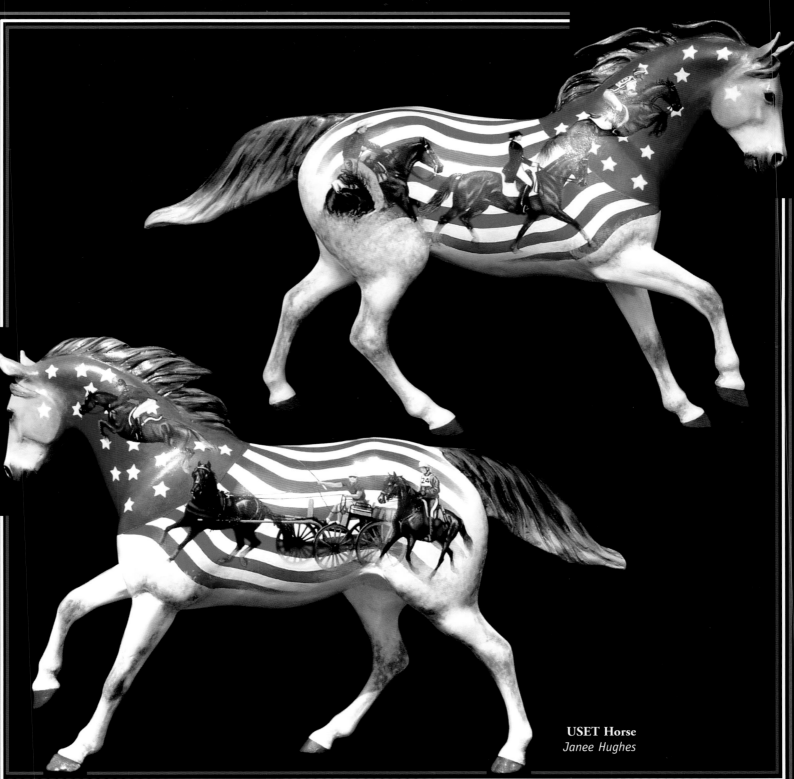

USET Horse
Janee Hughes

Fallen Heroes Memorial Pony
LD Burke, Ishmael Mena,
Shawn Pascuzzi, Bruce Hayles

Western Horses

From exploration to settlement, from ranch life to rodeos, when the tale of the American West has been told in paint there is usually a horse in the picture.

While the source of inspiration remains constant, the personal expression often takes us on a journey into an artistic frontier.

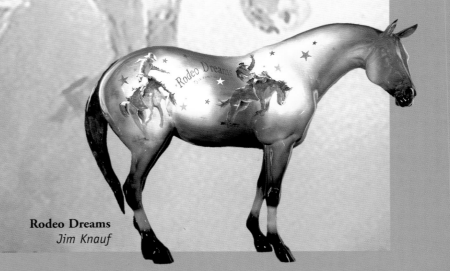

Rodeo Dreams
Jim Knauf

USDA: Ladies Choice
Lori Musil

Cowboy Working Horse
Sharon Higgins

Wild Women of the West
Patti Rooks

Blondes
David DeVary

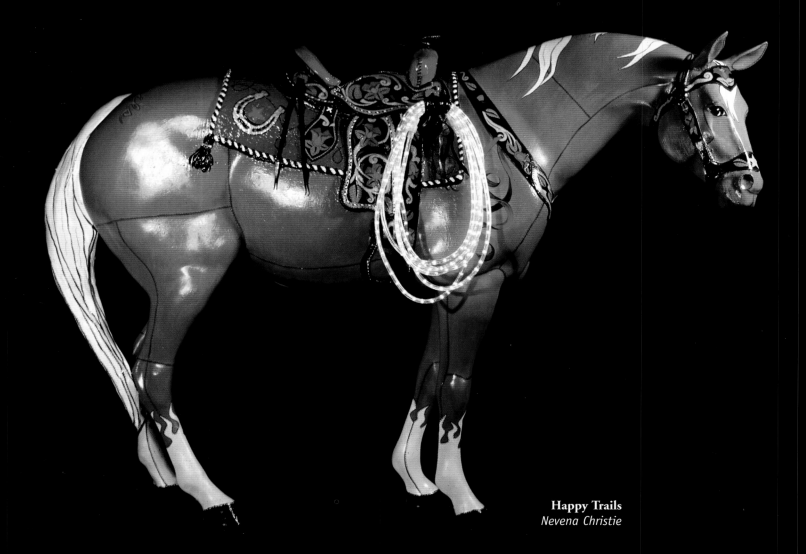

Happy Trails
Nevena Christie

Racehorses

Legs outstretched, tail and mane flowing, heads straining at the bit... images depicting the speed and power of running horses have been immortalized on canvas and in sculpture from the days in ancient Greece and Rome when chariot racing was a popular spectator sport, to the era when horseracing became "the sport of kings" and portraits of the most famous racehorses were prized, to picturesque interpretations by artists from The Trail of Painted Ponies.

Photo Finish
Janee Hughes

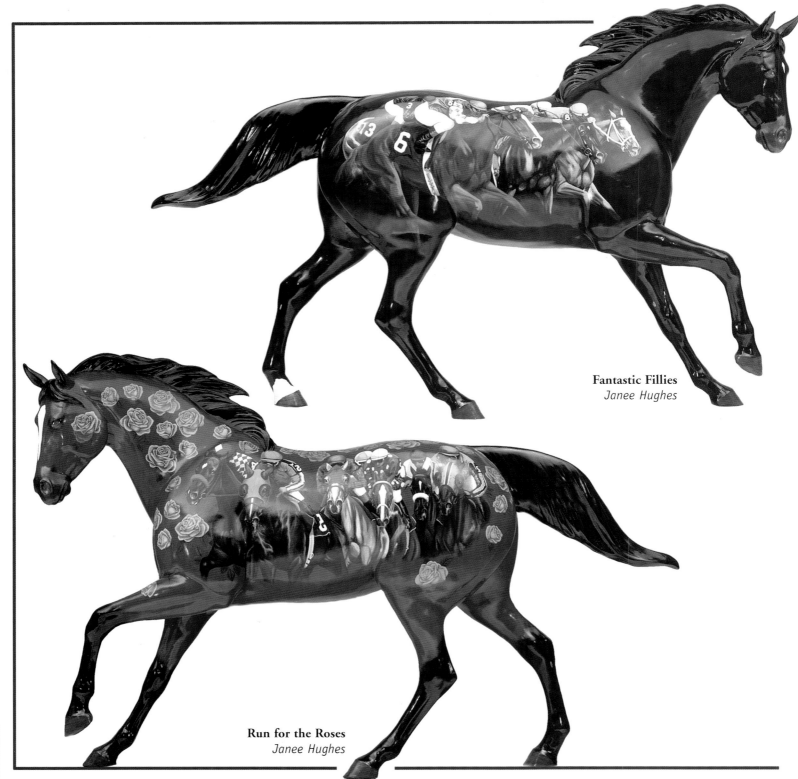

Fantastic Fillies
Janee Hughes

Run for the Roses
Janee Hughes

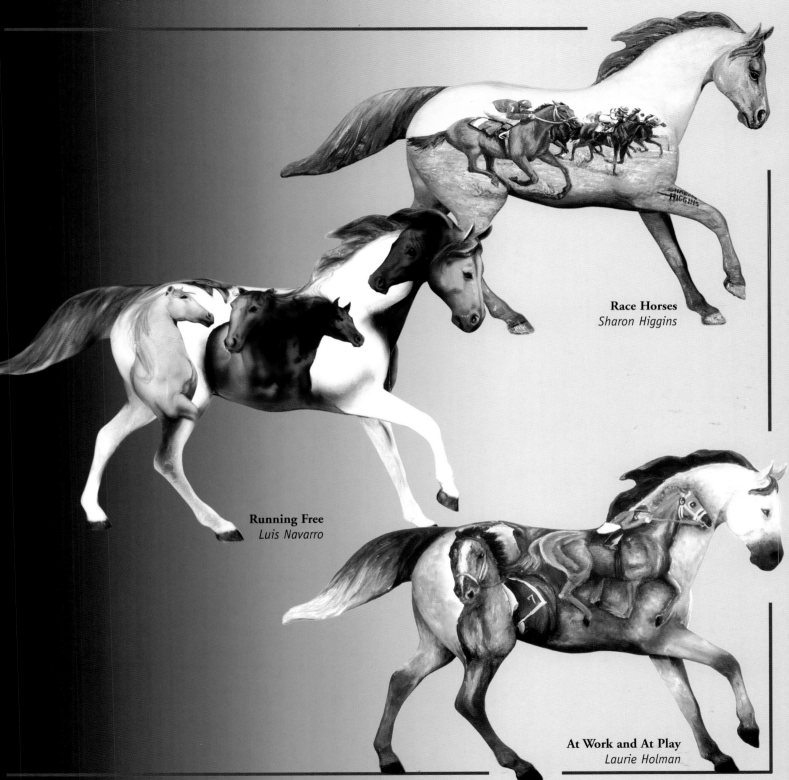

Race Horses
Sharon Higgins

Running Free
Luis Navarro

At Work and At Play
Laurie Holman

Great Expectations
Janee Hughes

Horse Power

For centuries the horse was a hardworking beast of burden, and a means of overland transportation. With the introduction of the steam engine its role in American life was diminished. But the term "horsepower" is still used to calculate the power of an engine, and horses continue to be a driving passion for artists.

Horsepower to Burn
Rich Mattson

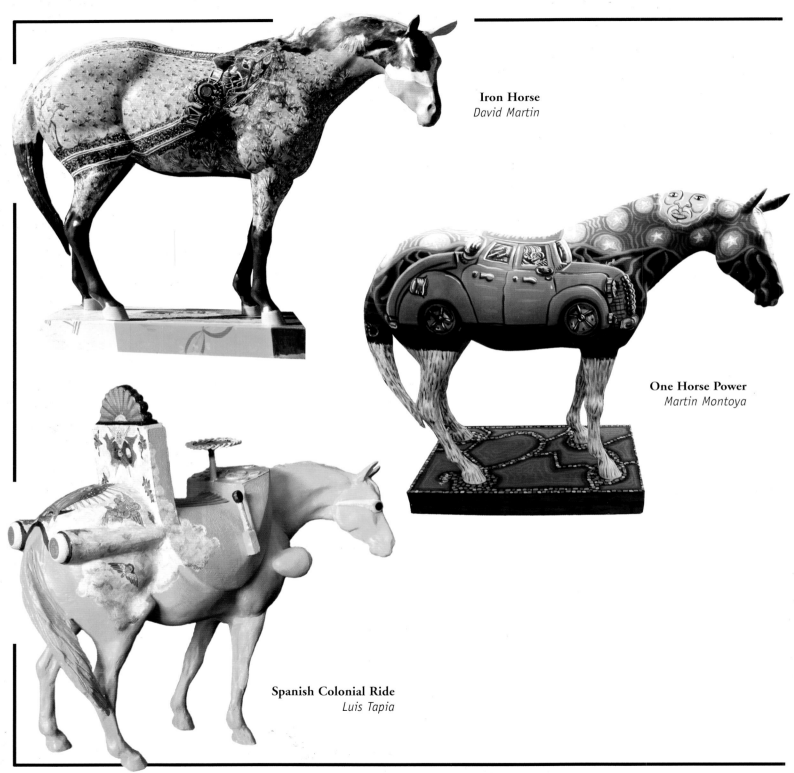

Iron Horse
David Martin

One Horse Power
Martin Montoya

Spanish Colonial Ride
Luis Tapia

Wound Up Time On The Range
Roger Evans

Hiway Roller
Dave Newman

Turbo Hay Burner
Brett Chromer

Motorcycle Mustang
David Losoya

Maverick Ponies

And then there are the wild horses that wear no brand.... the Ponies that are painted outside the lines and are impossible to round up into a single category... yet invite us to discover their beauty and mystery.

Five Card Stud
Gerri Mattson

Apple-oosa
Penny Thomas Simpson

Mosaic Appaloosa
Bob Coonts

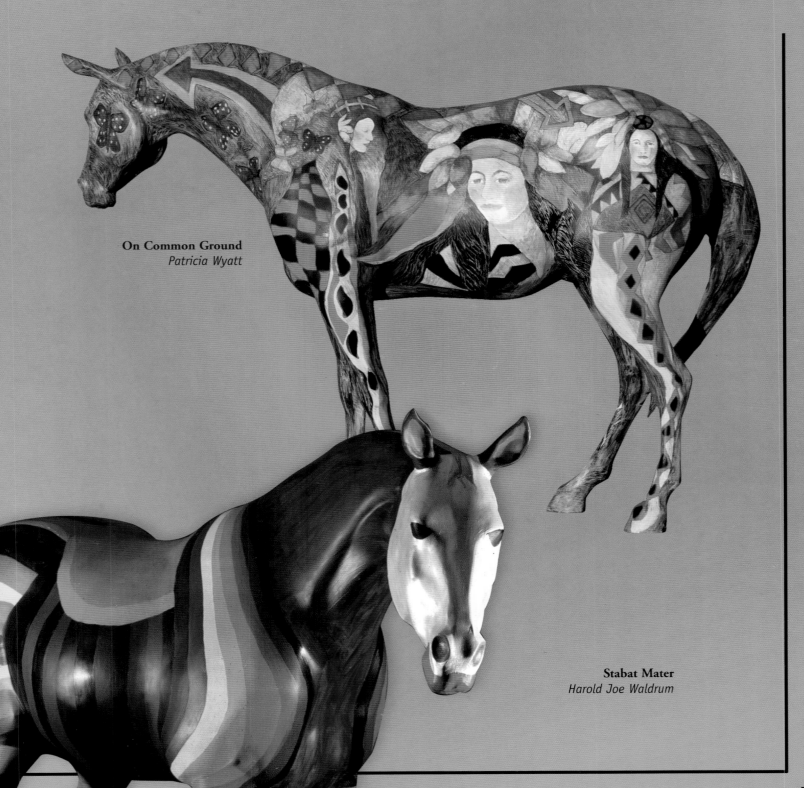

On Common Ground
Patricia Wyatt

Stabat Mater
Harold Joe Waldrum

Patrol Horse & Fireman Pony
A-1 Master Mold & Casting

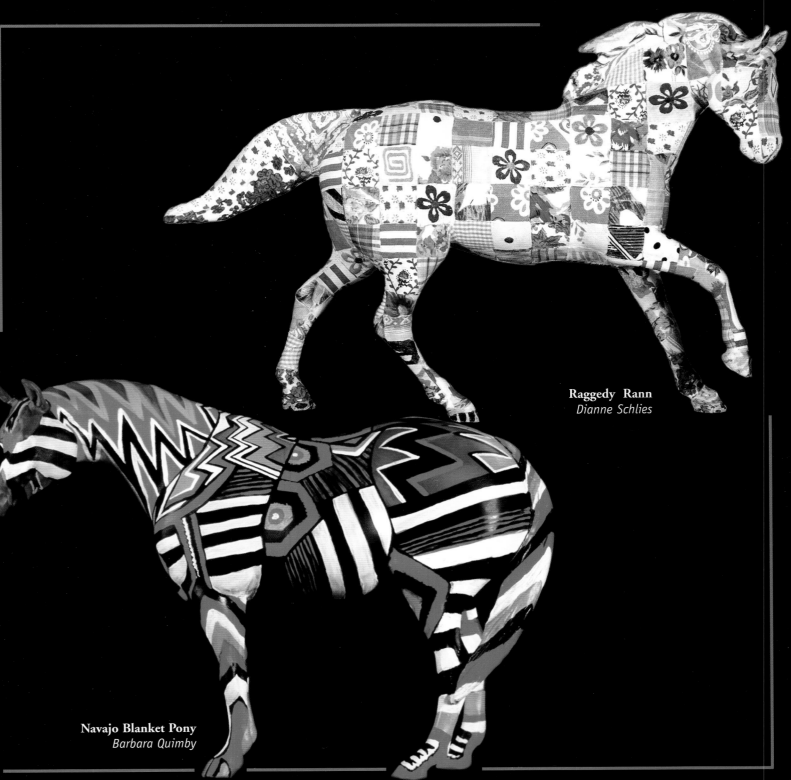

Raggedy Rann
Dianne Schlies

Navajo Blanket Pony
Barbara Quimby

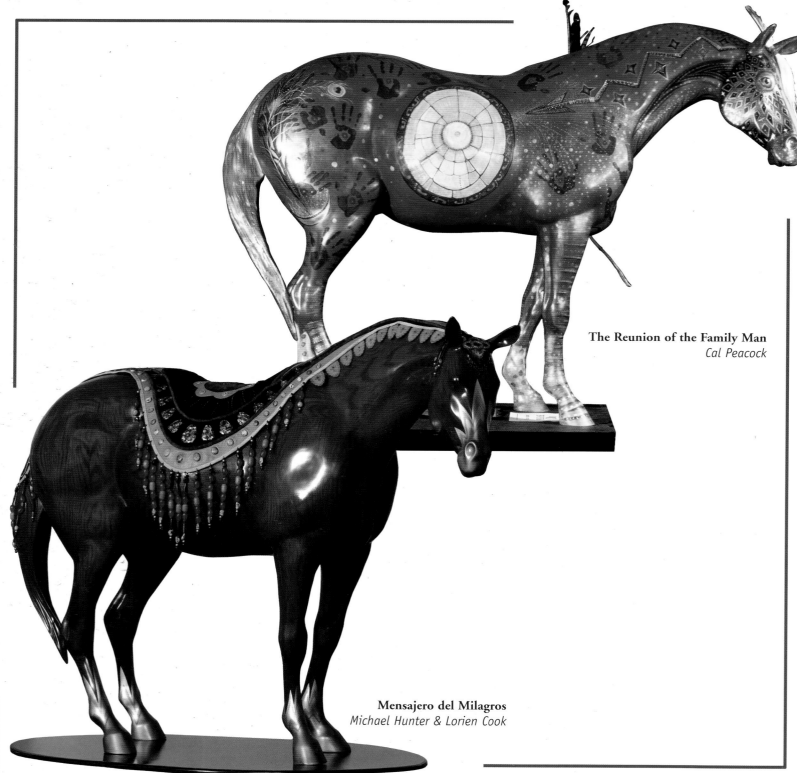

The Reunion of the Family Man
Cal Peacock

Mensajero del Milagros
Michael Hunter & Lorien Cook

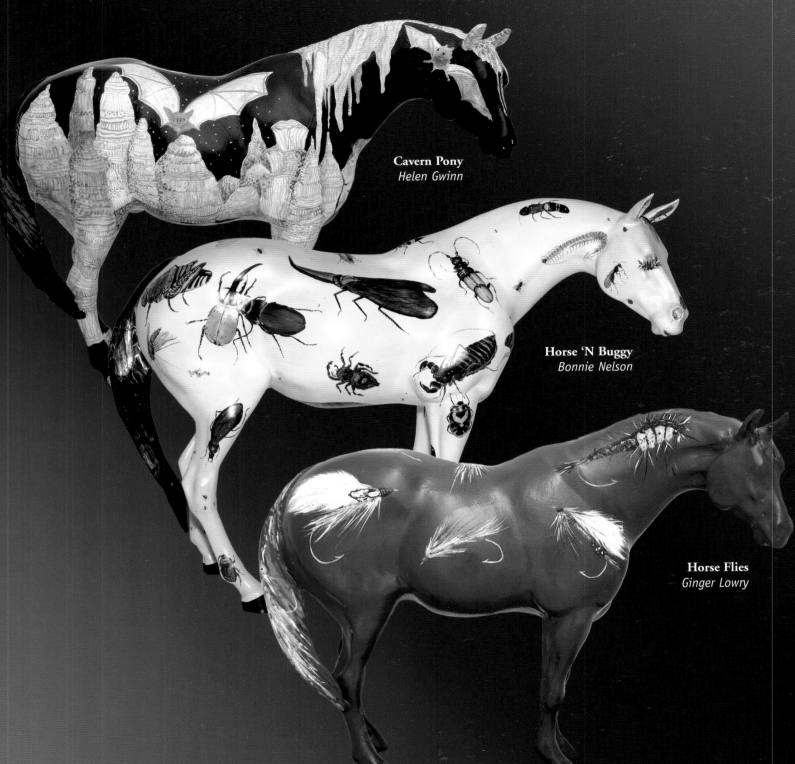

Cavern Pony
Helen Gwinn

Horse 'N Buggy
Bonnie Nelson

Horse Flies
Ginger Lowry

Caballo De Los Ojos
Anne Strait

Muy Caliente
Pat Beason

By the Dawn's Early Light
Jen Raynes

Trailblazer
John Nieto

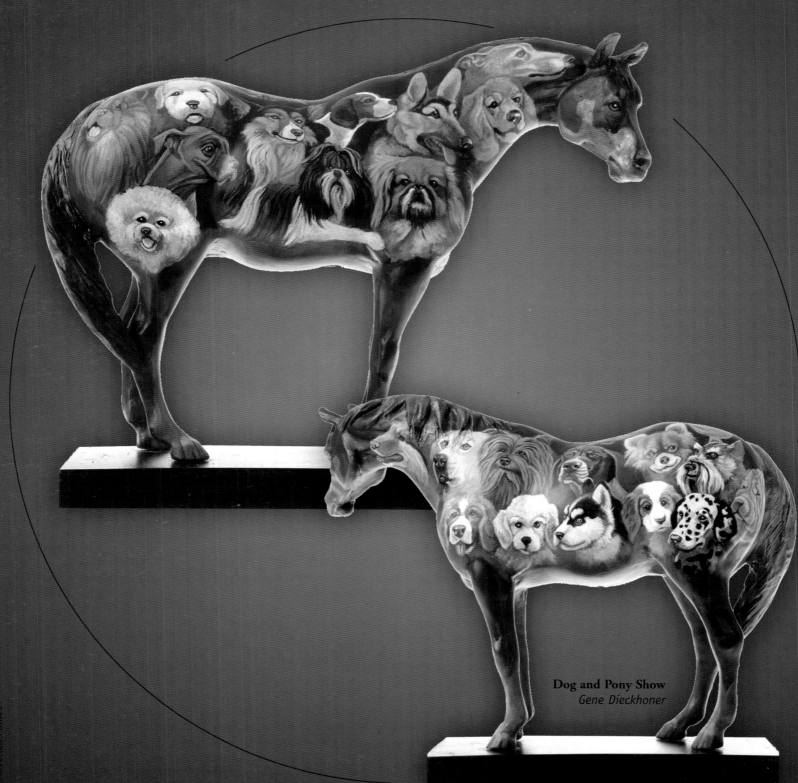

Dog and Pony Show
Gene Dieckhoner

Super Charger
Rod Barker

Chinese War Pony
Jeffrey Chan

Aloha Pony
Joel Nakamura

Buffalo Spirit
John Geryak

Buffalo Spirit
JOHN GERYAK

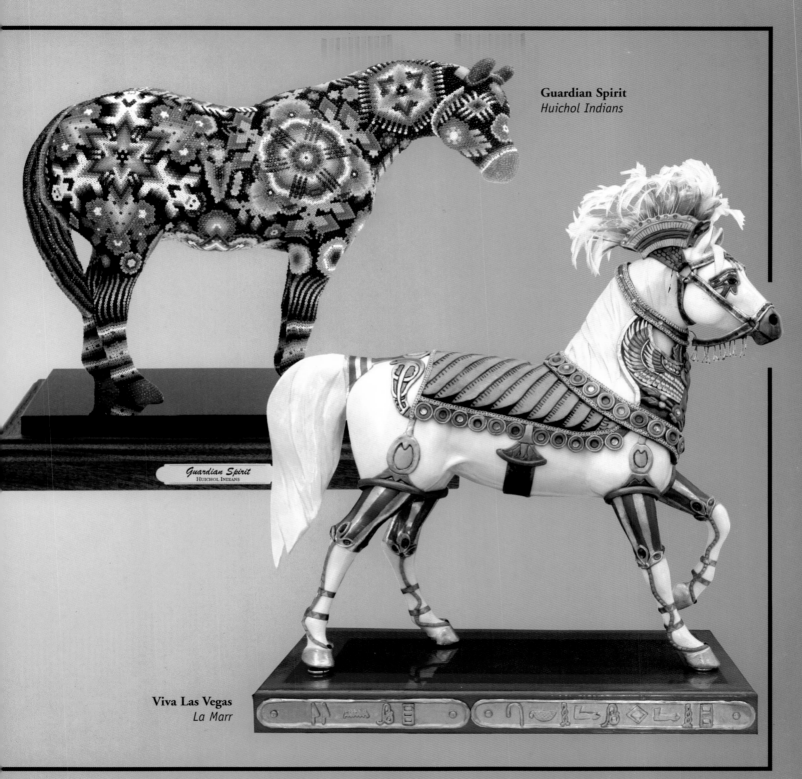

Guardian Spirit
Huichol Indians

Guardian Spirit
HUICHOL INDIANS

Viva Las Vegas
La Marr

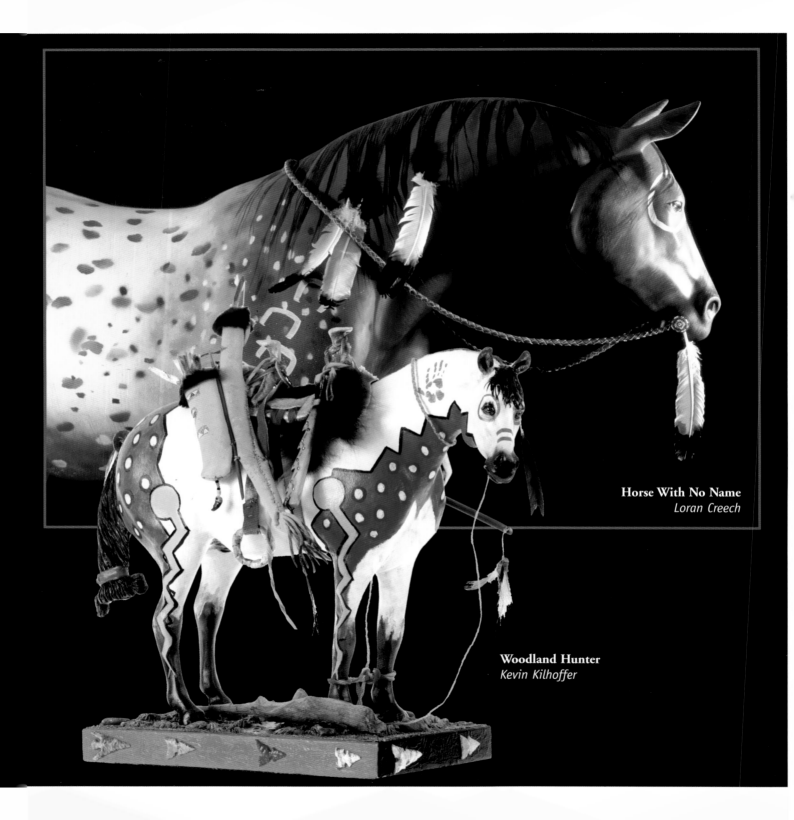

Horse With No Name
Loran Creech

Woodland Hunter
Kevin Kilhoffer

Ceremonial Pony
Cathy Smith & Star York

Crazy Horse
CJ Wells

Northern Lights
Janee Hughes

Facts, Figurines, and More Painted Pony Merchandise

The Trail of Painted Ponies originated in Santa Fe, New Mexico in 2001 as a public art project that invited the very best artists in the country to creatively transform life-size resin horse sculptures into stunningly original works of art. The power, beauty and magic of the Painted Ponies were enthusiastically recognized by millions of people, and the project garnered rave reviews in the national media. The Painted Ponies were then auctioned and sold, raising almost one million dollars for different philanthropic organizations.

Life-size 5'

Since that time, The Trail of Painted Ponies has continued to give artists the opportunity to express themselves creatively on smaller scale horse forms. Painted Pony "masterworks" stand almost 2 feet tall, are cast in bonded marble, and weigh approximately 30 pounds. Painted Pony maquettes are cast in resin and stand about one-foot tall. Distinguished by their uniqueness and the fantastic quality of the imagery, original one-of-a-kind Painted Pony artworks have sold to collectors and museums across the country.

24"

Masterwork

12"

Maquette

So popular are the Painted Ponies, that they have inspired a diverse line of merchandise that honors the original works of art. Painted Pony figurines, crafted with extraordinary attention to detail, have become one of the best-selling collectibles in America. Painted Pony jewelry, clothing and puzzles are artforms in their own right, and are available at amazingly affordable prices.

For more information: www.trailofpaintedponies.com

7"

Figurine

Kokopelli Pony

A sacred figure to Native tribes in the Southwest, the image of Kokopelli, a dancing hunchback playing a flute, appears most frequently in pottery and petroglyphs. A universal minstrel or music spirit who continues to fascinate people, even in our modern technological age, he is given a charming, contemporary interpretation by Joel Nakamura, an Asian-American artist known for his deep knowledge of tribal art and mythology.

Artist: Joel Nakamura

Caballito

Monument Valley, Spider Rock, Enchanted Mesa are names that evoke an aura of mystery and legends. Storied sites in the American Southwest, they also shape the dramatic backgrounds for the culturally rich imagery found in the paintings of Mexican/Yaqui artist Amado Pena. Using bold color, striking forms, dynamic composition, and the iconic faces that have distinguished his work for years, Pena has created, with his Pony, a tribute to the horses he has known, past and present.

Artist: Amado Pena

Saguaro Stallion

A former Creative Director with a New York marketing agency, John has enjoyed a successful second career in the arts after moving to Scottsdale, Arizona, where his paintings focus on highly personalized, contemporary interpretations of Nature. His extraordinary rendering of the wondrous effects of a moonrise and sunrise on a stand of saguaro cactus captures John's goal as a painter, which is "to offer new dimensions in how we see our one-of-a-kind desert landscape."

Artist: John Geryak

Epic Horse

Stone tablets have played an important role in the heritage of Chinese culture. Knowing this, Jeffrey Chan, an art designer for Hong Kong movies who also specializes in giftware design, conceived of a glossy black Pony on which a famous poem was carved in a manner that captured the beauty of the art of Chinese calligraphy. The poem, "Orchid Pavilion Preface," was written in 352 A.D. by Wang Xizhi, one of the most highly respected calligraphers/poets in Chinese history. It is a masterpiece that speaks to the happiness and grace of every living moment.

Artist: Jeffrey Chan

Incognito

Writes Janee Hughes, a former art teacher and book illustrator from Salem, Oregon, "Biologists are not in agreement about the purpose of a zebra's stripes. Some say the wonderful patterns act as camouflage in the tall grass, but others say the stripes confuse predators. When a lion sees a herd of zebras, it is difficult for her to distinguish one animal from another in order to single out a potential victim. Whichever the case may be, it was great fun creating a herd of Grant's zebras living 'Incognito.'"

Artist: Janee Hughes

Running with the Ancestors

"The inspiration for this Pony comes from prehistoric imagery found on European cave walls, where the grand drawings of horses were both magical and beautiful," says this painter, gallery director and teacher who founded the 5,000 Flowers Project, a national commemoration of 9/11 for healing and harmony through art. Just as contemporary horses echo the drawings of Stone Age artists, so does Carole feel she is linked to Paleolithic artists. "They are my ancestors of creativity and self-expression."

Artist: Carol Adamec
Sponsor: Jardin de los Ninos

CowPony

With millions of brushstrokes masterfully applied, Lori, a western and wildlife artist from Cerrillos, New Mexico, created an original, life-size Painted Pony that is proudly exhibited in the Booth Western Art Museum. Upon popular demand, it is now available as a figurine, and as a miniature retains the phenomenal creative power of the original. Sculpted into the Pony form as well as painted, a herd of Hereford cows emerge from the swelling muscles of the horse... and hidden among the red-and-whites, a savvy sorrel cowpony.

Artist: Lori Musil

Tropical Reef Horse

Seahorses come in an amazing variety of sizes and shapes, and have the ability to instantly change color, camouflaging themselves as seaweed or coral. By brilliantly covering her Pony with tropical fish, rendered realistically, overlapping and swimming in all directions, Laurie, a high school art teacher "in an isolated, dusty border town in far West Texas" who scuba dives as a hobby, has created a seahorse-of-a-different-color.

Artist: Laurie Holman

Skyrider

The Hopi believe that when their elders pass on they continue to exist among the clouds, where they protectively watch over their descendants. Wendy, a graduate of the London School of Fine Art who feels her spirit dwells in the deserts, mesas and canyons of the Southwest, has taken this belief to new heights, literally, imagining a Pony stampeding across the sky on a glorious journey, collecting the faces of the ancestors and becoming one with the Cloud People.

Artist: Wendy Wells-Bailey

Fallen Heroes Memorial Pony

There could be no more deserving example, in modern times, of bravery and heroic conduct than the firemen and policemen who pay the ultimate price while keeping the rest of us out of harm's way. Drawing on traditional imagery observed at the funerals of military heroes – a riderless horse with a pair of empty, high-top boots fitted in the stirrups backwards - The Trail of Painted Ponies, in collaboration with assorted artisans and craftsmen, created this emotionally stirring and uniquely American tribute to these Fallen Heroes.

Artist: The Trail of Painted Ponies

Willing

Often referred to as one of the most imaginative and compelling ceramists of his generation, Virgil lives and works at the Cochiti Pueblo. He is known as much for taking traditional art forms in cutting-edge directions, as collaborative clothing ventures with New York fashion designer Donna Karan. Tattooed with traditional pottery designs before it was strapped down in black leather and silver spikes, this dramatic re-interpretation of Black Beauty has a mystique, a sensuality and a power that is vintage Virgil Ortiz.

Artist: Virgil Ortiz

Reunion of the Family of Man

Artist Cal Peacock's painted tin "Medicine Horses" have been displayed in such prestigious venues as the Smithsonian Museum. But she considers "Reunion" the "king of the herd." Intricately covered with amazingly detailed imagery and symbols that express empathy and compassion towards our fellow man, and carrying a medicine bundle stocked with bird feathers, Cal's gorgeous Pony is an expression of the importance of soulfully connecting with Nature.

Artist: Cal Peacock
Sponsor: Painted Pinto Farms

Painted Lady

"Painted Ladies" is a term often applied to resplendent Victorian houses, brightly painted and expertly restored. Armed with this knowledge, New Mexico artist Barbara Quimby cleverly conceived of a Painted Lady Pony, a dolled-up equine celebration of the Victorian spirit as it lives today.

Artist: Barbara Quimby
Sponsor: Citizen's Committee for Historical Preservation in Las Vegas, New Mexico

Reindeer Roundup

In hopes of drawing Santa's sleigh through the Christmas sky like the red-nosed Rudolph, this reindeer-wannabe tried to disguise the fact he was a Painted Pony by rounding up a set of antlers and throwing a gaudy saddle blanket on his back that lights up the night with stars. Even if he doesn't get a chance to pull Santa's sleigh, he will bring cheer to the season, and make this a memorable Christmas for those who find him prancing under their tree.

Artist: Mike Dowdall and Joy Steuerwald

Horsefeathers

Nobody seems to know the derivation of the term "horsefeathers." The most likely explanation is it began as a sanitized variant of "horse hooey", used to express the view that something is unlikely, about as improbable as that pigs might fly... or that horses should have feathers. By adorning her Pony with large, multi-colored feathers, this former art teacher from Texas has given the term a totally new form of expression.

Artist: Jeanne Selby

Happy Holidays

Think Christmas on the ranch... tacking up your trusty horse with a seasonal saddle blanket, tying on stockings instead of saddlebags and buckling up a breast collar that tinkles like sleigh bells... then riding over to the neighbor's cabin to share hearth and home. Could there be a better way to spread holiday cheer? Joy Steuerwald and Mike Dowdall, designers at Westland Giftware, didn't think so when they created "Happy Holidays."

Artist: Mike Dowdall and Joy Steuerwald

Rodeo Dreams

A cover artist whose Cowboy paintings massage, twist and tweak traditional concepts of Western art at the same time they embrace Western iconography, Jim lets his Painted Pony speak for himself: "I don't want to plough or amble along a trail. I'm not built for dressage and I'm certainly nobody's pet. Give me center stage and I'll give you a show because I'm Rodeo Dreams."

Artist: Jim Knauf
Sponsor: Margot MacDougall

The Magician

In certain plains Indian tribes there was a special tribal figure who spoke to and for the horses. He was believed to possess supernatural powers, and called The "Magician." As rendered by Taos artist Andersen Kee, who was born on the Navajo Reservation and whose mother was a weaver and father a silversmith, the "Magician" is releasing a herd of multi-colored spirit Ponies from the inside of his elkskin robe, and then gathering them on the backside.

Artist: Andersen Kee
Sponsor: Ken and Barb Hummel

American Dream Horse

Asked by a Christian ministry that places Russian orphans in the homes of loving families to paint a Pony that captures the dream-come-true that awaits these children in America, Bonny incorporated the warm red and deep gold colors associated with Russian matruska dolls, along with children's faces peering out with hopeful expressions, doves of peace, and flowers and leaves, into a spectacular artwork that makes a powerful statement about the great freedom in life's journey.

Artist: Bonny
Sponsor: International Guardian Angels Outreach

Native People's Pony

"As an artist, I have always had this vision of different cultures around the world coming together sharing their beliefs, customs, blending as one on this small planet we call Mother Earth," says Frank Salcido, a Navajo from the Standing House Clan, living in Portland Oregon. With both sides of his Pony's face represented by Aztec and Mayan warriors, adorned with tribal figures from an Australian Aborigine to an African Masai woman, Frank has fulfilled his artistic mission of using positive themes to contemporarily showcase traditional lifestyles.

Artist: Frank Salcido

Big Red

A culturally diverse and worldly fellow, Santa has many interpretations and different names: Father Christmas in England, Kriss Kringle in Germany, Pere Noel in France, Saint Nicholas in the Netherlands. But almost universally he is a plump and jolly figure who dresses in red, carries a bulging sack on his back, and brings gifts to good children. Destined to become a classic, "Big Red" is a lavish and loving example of how the symbol of Christmas is no longer just a decorated Christmas tree, but is now all about artistic expression.

Artist: The Trail of Painted Ponies Design Department

Fetish Pony

To Native Americans, a fetish is any object that possesses "spirit power." They believe that when the object is treated with respect, the spirit that resides within can bring its owner good luck, good health and a harmonious life. With this in mind, Oregon painter Lynn Bean created an extraordinary "fetish pony" on which the spirit images of different horses seem to emerge from inside a sandstone carving of a host horse, who wears a "power pack" of feathers, beads and shells on its back.

Artist: Lynn Bean

Deck the Halls

Imagine a Painted Pony spruced up as a Christmas tree in fresh greenery, decorated with vintage Christmas ornaments and red bows, strung with tinsel garland and multi-colored lights, and posed on a Christmas skirt that sparkles like a magic carpet. That's what the Design Department of The Trail of Painted Ponies had in mind when it created a seasonal selection that captures the Christmas Magic expressed in the carol, "Deck the Halls."

Artist: The Trail of Painted Ponies Design Department

Year of the Horse

Painted in conjunction with the Chinese "Year of the Horse", this western and wildlife artist from Cerrillos, NM created a classic celebration of the different horse breeds of America. From the American Quarter Horse to the Thoroughbred, Appaloosa and American Paint, ten horses move gracefully and majestically across the curves and bulges of the original sculpture, each exhibiting a personality of its own, with a style and flair that is Lori's personal hallmark.

Artist: Lori Musil

Silver Lining

In Greek mythology, Pegasus is regarded as the horse of the Muses, and has always been at the service of poets. And so the story is told of a handsome youth who jumped on the back of a horse that unfolded the splendor of a mighty set of wings and soared towards the heavens... where he can still be seen as the star constellation, Pegasus. Santa Fe sculptor and horsewoman Star Liana York created the original, crystal-eyed interpretation of the legendary flying steed to benefit a therapeutic horseback riding program.

Artist: Star Liana York

Super Charger

In the 15th Century, when knights were defenders of the faith, a woman's honor, or just about anything that endowed them with greater glory, so did their "chargers" share in the accolades. In fact, the exalted association between man and horse is precisely what is meant by chivalry - an adaptation of the French word meaning horse, cheval. With this in mind, Rod Barker, executive director of The Trail of Painted Ponies, designed a "super-charger" fit for the noblest of knights.

Artist: Rod Barker

Gift Horse

In celebration of the way Painted Ponies have become the perfect gift for holidays, birthdays and anniversaries, we asked Misty, an artist from Columbus, Ohio who is a member of League of Animal Artists, to create a Pony that would be appropriate for every gift-giving 1 occasion. Standing on a beautifully wrapped purple package, dressed with cakes, party hats, streamers, balloons and presents, and wearing a candy-colored halter, "Gift Horse" is a virtual Painted Pony party that is as much fun as it is innovative.

Artist: Misty Lynn Auld

Blondes

David DeVary is one of an emerging group of so-called "New West" artists who celebrate the myths of the American West. His oil and gold-leaf paintings, boldly colored and dramatically toplit, present contemporary cowboys and cowgirls in the guise of romanticized American icons. Posed like glamorous fashion models on the sides of a beautiful Palomino, their eyes shadowed by a low-tipped cowboy hat, the women on this Pony intentionally glorify the freedom and self-confidence we associate with "the cowgirl."

Artist: David DeVary

Horsepower to Burn

He came of age in the '50s, when hotrods and drag racing were "cool," when flames and checkered flags were stock images in car magazines. Years later, after three-decades teaching art and coaching basketball and winning an award as the New Mexico Art Educator of the year in 1988, Rich would draw on those times, those memories, when he was encouraged to paint a Pony by a NASCAR fan.

Artist: Rich Mattson
Sponsor: Best Western Guadalupe Inn, White City, NM

Dream Warriors

"My best designs come to me when I am quiet," says Colorado artist Ross Lampshire, perhaps best known as a rodeo photographer and potter. "An image or idea enters my mind almost as a whisper... and fast takes on a life of its own." Inspired by written accounts of Sitting Bull's dreams prior to battle, Ross had his own dream one night of Sitting Bull silhouetted against a full moon with clouds parting, as if in search of a vision. Working in a stylized manner, Ross has created a dramatic, powerful and flowing design that honors this famous Sioux chief.

Artist: Ross Lampshire

Woodland Hunter

"Woodland Hunter came to me through research and study of the northern plains tribes," says Kevin Kilhoffer, a native of western Oklahoma who studies, draws and paints the American West. "I found records of a Franciscan missionary stationed at a fur trade fort dating back to 1836, and in his notes he described a Teton Sioux warrior who rode into the fort wearing a magnificent war shirt adorned with scalps and wonderful art work decorating his horse." Incorporating markings that tell of deeds, wisdom, wealth and bravery, and outfitting his Pony with a shield, weapons, saddle and bags for transporting food, Kevin has created an astounding and historically accurate tribute to that Plains Indian warrior.

Artist: Kevin Kilhoffer

Horse With No Name

A story is told about a riderless Appaloosa, flamboyantly painted with symbols that portray a warrior's bravery during battle, wandering the prairie as if in search of his master. According to this tale, the horse would never let anyone else ride him, though many tried. The lightning bolt on his face, the sun on his shoulder, the circle around his eye, the handprint on his flank, the feathers in his mane and tail marked him as a horse with powerful medicine. And so he was allowed to roam the plains freely... to be eventually memorialized by New Mexico artist Loran Creech.

Artist: Loran Creech

Spirits of the Northwest

Animals are important to the Northwest Native cultures. Using bold colors and designs based on the Haida and Tlingit styles of art, Laurie Holman, who lives and teaches art in Alaska, presents us with various animal totems featured in traditional Alaskan stories: the Raven, Grizzly Bear, Salmon, Eagle, and Whale. "I wanted them to cover the entire Pony, like a puzzle, with all of the pieces telling the great story of life, death and rebirth."

Artist: Laurie Holman

Guardian Spirit

Deer and wolves that speak to man, arrows that carry prayers, serpents that bring rain - are all real in the Huichol Indian belief system. The Huichol live in the Sierra Madre Mountains of central Mexico, and for centuries these spiritual people have been beading decorative items to use as offerings to the gods. Their world is rich in symbolism and imagination, and they encode their spiritual knowledge through their art. The Trail of Painted Ponies was honored when a Huichol couple agreed to create an original Pony intricately beaded with images that represent life and enlightenment.

Artists: The Huichol Indians

Dog and Pony Show

If you love dogs, you have come to the right place. Sedona wildlife artist Gene Dieckhoner - whose noteworthy accomplishments include serving as Art Director for Fox Animation Studios - has created a delightful tribute to our "faithful friends." Pure breeds and mixed breeds alike are gathered together on the form of a horse - another companion animal - that itself has been painted to resemble a Doberman Pinscher. For the dog and horse lover, this Pony is the next best thing to owning your own!

Artist: Gene Dieckhoner

Many Tribes

Pottery is one of the oldest art forms in the Native American culture, and each tribe has a style which is traditionally its own. Today, however, tribal potters borrow or copy designs and techniques from each other. Drawing on the diverse animal and geometric patterns found on many authentic pots, Linda, a Delaware Indian living in Las Vegas, has painted a Pony wrapped in the traditional and contemporary ceramic designs of many tribes.

Artist: Linda Hassett

Vi's Violet Vision

There are personal reasons why this artist prefers to be known by the moniker, Mister E. They are suggested in the poem he provided in place of a biography: "Adopted here, adopted there. So many names, not one my own. A father a day, not one there to stay." Though his identity remains a "mystery," his talent is evident and extraordinary. From award-winning oil portraits to comic book illustrations, with this tribute to Carousel Horses, this artist is making a new name for himself.

Artist: Mister E
Sponsor: DeVargas Mall

Mosaic Appaloosa

After distinguishing himself in the field of graphic design in Colorado, Bob established a national name for himself in the fine art field with a signature style that borders on the abstract, yet reflects a true image. "I look at animals and try to strategically place color and design elements that help define their anatomy in a different way." His paintings are part of permanent museum collections in Poland, Finland, Germany and Japan, and were displayed in special shows at the White House and Smithsonian Institution.

Artist: Bob Coonts
Sponsor: Catherine Cox

Happy Trails

A former fashion designer from New York City, Nevena wanted to create a horse that reflected the style and costumes worn by Gene Autry and Roy Rogers - '30s and '40s cowboy retro, in other words. It's no mistake that her Pony looks as if it is fashioned out of tooled leather, with a vintage saddle cinched on its back. Nevena now lives in El Paso and runs Rocketbuster Boot Company, where some of the wildest cowboy boots you will ever see are handmade.

Artist: Nevena Christi
Sponsor: Back at the Ranch

Renewal of Life

Natasha's travels abroad and around the Southwest have fueled her love for interpreting the "magical landscapes" she has witnessed. A dawn seen through mists hovering over the Rio Grande River that flows through a bird sanctuary in southern New Mexico, inspired this work of art. Whether she is painting on a canvas or a Pony, this artist has a unique ability to create a spiritual luminescence that invites the viewer to enter a meditative space that seems to live inside her art.

Artist: Natasha Isenhour
Sponsor: Socorro Chamber of Commerce

QuarterHorse

Experimenting with the design and dimensionality of an actual quarter, and the sculptural form of the horse breed that goes by the same name, this former Art Director for a national magazine found the coin's features lent themselves to the existing contours of the horse. "I particularly like how the eagle's wings flow into the horse's mane and tail," Kathy says. "By focusing on the eagle and selected words of a quarter, it also offers an opportunity to reflect an additional theme of national allegiance." A silver finish, appearing "aged" for contrast, gives the appearance of the horse a feeling of having been crafted from metal.

Artist: Kathy Morawski
Sponsor: The Trail of Painted Ponies

Give Me Wings

Many of the Painted Ponies carry messages or themes, and this is one for our time. It was inspired by a poem Kathy wrote after the events of September 11: "I will not forget those who sacrificed on the altar of freedom. Precious freedom, give me wings to soar beyond my dreams and touch the stars." As a child of the Southwest, the artist was raised on the San Carlos Apache Reservation and Pine Ridge Sioux Reservation, where her father trained Indian police forces.

Artist: Kathy Morrow -
Sponsor: High Desert Bank

Sequintial: A Sequine

Nancy, who has a Fine Arts Degree from the Kansas City Art Institute, is known as a collage artist who artfully incorporates found objects into her artwork, usually in some sort of repeating pattern. "I can't throw out junk mail without first removing the canceled stamps," she says, by way of explaining how she came to cover her horse with 77,000 iridescent and multi-colored sequins.

Artist: Nancy Fleming
Sponsor: Minnie Wright

Rosie the Apparoosa

This work of radiant and unusual beauty was created by a New Mexico artist nationally known for using the floral form as a means for exploring the relationships of color and value in painting. Riotous displays of multi-hued roses in bud and bloom, with not a single flower repeated, sprout from earthen hooves and thorny branch-covered legs. "I dubbed her Rosie," says Marianne, "and as she departed her first stable on a warm day in May, three real rose bushes by my studio door bloomed more profusely than any past spring."

Artist: Marianne Hornbuckle
Sponsor: Santa Fe Youth Symphony

Go van Gogh

This tribute to the Dutch master, which combines two of his most recognizable paintings with a humorous rendition of his facial appearance, complete with a missing ear, was created by the sculptor who designed the actual horse forms used in The Trail of Painted Ponies art project. As talented at painting as she is at sculpting, Star, who also breeds horses on her New Mexico ranch, knows her horses, and playfully named this piece after the famous racehorse, Go Man Go.

Artist: Star Liana York
Sponsor: The Trail of Painted Ponies

Unity

It was not solely for his grand vision - combining imagery of the early Spanish explorers who brought the horse to America five centuries ago, with representations of the Native tribes whose culture was radically changed by the horse - that this former fashion photographer turned pop artist received the award for the most ambitious Pony. To give his artwork monumental impact, Georges Monfils covered it with over a million and a half tiny Indian seed beads, applied one at a time! So impressive was the outcome, which took the artist over 1,400 hours to complete, that it was nominated for the Guinness Book of World Records.

Artist: Georges Monfils
Sponsor: The Sylvia Toth Foundation

Patrol Horse

Although there is a historical relationship between horses and law enforcement - think Royal Canadian Mounted Police and Texas Rangers - the partnership today is limited primarily to search and rescue missions, and crowd control. Nevertheless, out of respect for tradition, the creative team of Dwayne and Ginger Ulibarri has created a "poster mount," smartly tacking up their Pony in an officer's uniform, polished black boots, campaign hat, mirrored shades, and the classic imperturbable expression that makes you wonder if he has eyes in the back of his head. Nothing is going to rock this Pony's world!

Artist: Dwayne and Ginger Ulibarri
Sponsor: A-1 Master Mold and Casting Services

On Common Ground

The unity and harmony of the feminine spirit resound in the vibrant art of California-raised Patricia Wyatt. As with her paintings, her Pony tells a story that speaks to the timeless themes of companionship and the collective power, wisdom and beauty of women around the world. Animals and lush flowering plants surround the figures on the artist's Pony, emblems of the natural world that pay tribute to the Earth, whose mysterious power awakens us all to life and connects all things.

Artist: Patricia Wyatt
Sponsor: The Trail of Painted Ponies

War Pony

Comanche artist Rance Hood is one of the most recognized names in Southwest Art. His paintings, known for their drama and authenticity, hang in museums and corporate collections. The opportunity to recreate a traditional war pony, complete with a buffalo pelt saddle, lance-and-shield, arrows and feathers, became the pinnacle piece of his distinguished career.

Artist: Rance Hood
Sponsor: Rance Hood Gallery

Route 66 Horse

Ellen Sokoloff considers herself an "Americana painter." Her artwork preserves scenes from an earlier time in our country's history. Childhood memories of western trips along historic Route 66, America's "Mother Road", inspired the collage of diners, motels, gas stations and tourist attractions that embellish her Painted Pony.

Artist: Ellen Sokoloff
Sponsor: Gulfstream Worldwide

Fireman Pony

Horses were an important part of the early Fire Services, hauling water wagons to the scene of burning buildings and houses. Cleverly, and with humor and affection, Dwayne and Ginger Ulibarri have captured that sense of the horse as a fireman's best friend. As well as being artists in their own right, the Ulibarri's operate the Albuquerque foundry where the Painted Pony forms are cast.

Artist: Dwayne & Ginger Ulibarri
Sponsor: A-1 Master Mold & Casting Service

Wildfire

Anyone who has lived in the West knows firsthand about the awesome power and unpredictability of a wildfire. As well, anyone who has ridden horses knows they too are powerful and can be unpredictable. Carlsbad artist Gerri Mattson has creatively combined these two natural forces into a single dynamic image in which a forest fire raging out of control and horse stand together in a single artform.

Artist: Gerri Mattson
Sponsor: Randy & Meg Milligan

Boot Scootin' Horsey

Carla Slusher lives on a ranch in southeastern New Mexico where she paints to country-and-western music. As her vision of a dancing horse wearing a cowboy hat, jeans, and color-coordinated boots, ready for a night on the town, neared completion, it so happened that her favorite radio station played the song "Boot Scootin' Boogie." This is how she came up with the name for her Pony, which has attitude with a capital A.

Artist: Carla Slusher
Sponsor: Century 21 Associated Professionals

Navajo Blanket Pony

After receiving a degree from the Boston Museum School of Fine Art, New Englander Barbara Tomasko Quimby moved to Wagon Mound, New Mexico, where she fell in love with the native cultures and people of the West. Admiring the artistry displayed by Navajo women weaving fabulous blankets with thread on loom, she was moved to create this tribute, incorporating the color and design "of day and night, of deserts flat and mountain height."

Artist: Barbara Tomasko Quimby
Sponsor: HorsePower New Mexico

Caballo Brillante

Roger Montoya is a nationally recognized renaissance figure, as well known for his dance performances as his landscape paintings. He served as Artistic Director of this Pony, assembling a team of some 50 people, ranging in age from 5 to 81, from a New Mexico village to collect glass and ceramic shards from nearby riverbeds and old dumps, and arrange them into a mosaic that danced with light and color.

Artist: Roger Montoya
Sponsor: Good Hands Gallery

Lightning Bolt Colt

In Lakota Sioux mythology the horse is a Thunder Being who brings storms to Mother Earth. With storms come rain and change. With this in mind, Choctaw artist Dyanne Strongbow imagined a thuderstorm centered in the horse's hindquarters, breaking up as it moved toward his head into the sunny skies of a new day.

Artist: Dyanne Strongbow
Sponsor: Renee Ingold

Karuna (Compassion, in Sanskrit)

Says actress and animal-lover Ali MacGraw, "I chose to make a fantasy creature, inspired by the fabulous horses of Central Asia, that would inspire compassion for all God's creatures, great and small, all over the world." With Karuna, which means "Compassion" in Sanskrit, Ali demonstrates that her talent and creativity extend far beyond the silver screen.

Artist: Ali MacGraw
Sponsor: Santa Fe Animal Shelter & Humane Society

Five Card Stud

Artistic inspiration comes in many forms. Drawing on her experience as a secondary art teacher, Carlsbad artist Gerri Mattson gave herself an assignment. She made a list of words that related to horses, and then began to sketch out corresponding ideas. The word "Stud" prompted an association with poker, which led to a horse fancifully adorned with gaming, casino, and lottery images.

Artist: Gerri Mattson
Sponsor: Dorothy Queen & The Carlsbad Foundation

Motorcycle Mustang

A second-generation lover and owner of motorcycles, David Losoya, an airbrush artist from Artesia, New Mexico, wanted to create a creature that, "If I was a biker in the 19th century, I would ride." With the help of friends and family, he molded many parts of real motorcycles onto his horse, including mufflers, a kickstarter, leather saddlebags, and chains instead of reins. This Pony rumbles!

Artist: David Losoya
Sponsor: Yates Petroleum Corporation

Spirit War Pony

The Santa Fe artist Tavlos is credited with originating the famous howling coyote imagery that become a trademark of Southwest art in the '80s. Known for his bold colors and vivid designs, he took a pop art approach to the Native American tradition of painting their war horses, giving his Pony a turquoise coat and decorating it with dazzling accents.

Artist: Tavlos
Sponsor: Bill & Mary Lynn Oliver

Children of the Garden

This delightful creation by a "tile artist" who designs handmade tiles (www.elkabodetile.com) tells a story of children racing across a magical garden on the back of a magical horse. A place where, in the artist's words, "For a magical moment the 'real world' was not allowed to encroach." On the original Pony, the children, bugs and flowers were all formed in clay and fired for hardness before they were hand painted.

Artist: Connie Garcia
Sponsor: Jardin de los Ninos

Sky of Enchantment

After completing her studies in art, music and fashion design in Hamburg, Germany, Ilse lived in South Africa and Spain before finding paradise in the tiny New Mexico village of Magdalena. There, Ilse writes, "one is blessed with amazingly wide horizons during the day and unrivaled clear views of the stars, milky way and other galaxies at night." Adorned with gold celestial formations that sparkle with semi-precious gems, her Pony epitomizes the artist's gift for creating original and enchanting artworks.

Artist: Ilse Magener
Sponsor: None

Dances with Hooves

This Santa Fe folk artist is known for paintings and sculpture that blend Native American and aboriginal styles with a contemporary art sensibility. Ty has blanketed his Pony with intricate petroglyph and pictograph designs that seem to float on a rock-like background. "The initial impact is of a textual nature, but upon closer viewing, if one focuses on each design element as a vignette, as a picture all its own, there is much more for the viewer to explore."

Artist: Ty Anderle
Sponsor: None

Tewa Horse

Born to a family of artists and craftsmen from the Tesuque Pueblo in New Mexico, Tom (a tribal policeman) wanted to incorporate some of the traditional images that have been handed down from generation to generation, into a design that was contemporary in feeling and rich with symbolism. To do this, he combined various animal abstractions with geometric patterns. The sash represents good fortune. The blanket honors the horse as a bold and strong being. The eagle is a symbol of prosperity. The handprint stands for the loving touch of all creation.

Artist: Tom Tapia
Sponsor: The New Mexican newspaper

Blue Medicine

A gifted writer and painter, this Cherokee artist wanted her Pony to stand not only as a work of art, but an "expression of healing and support for those in need in our community." Adorned with a tribal sash made of leather, shells and beads, decorated with individual handprints of children, Mary worked overtime to complete this "vision and personal prayer" before passing to the other side in the summer of 2003.

Artist: Mary Iron Eyes
Sponsor: David Stanridge

Wound Up Time On The Range

An architect who wanted to design buildings in the Frank Lloyd Wright tradition - who wanted to work outside the lines, in other words - for many years Roger made his living as a draftsman, translating architectural designs into three-dimension illustrations. As an escape, he turned to humorous sculpture. By placing a little boy wearing a ten-gallon Stetson on the back of a Pony painted to look like a Southwestern landscape, and adding wheels to the base and a cord with a ball at the end, Roger has transformed his Painted Pony into a child's pull toy.

Artist: Roger Evans
Sponsor: The Range Cafe

Ghost Horse

A Mohican Indian from northern Wisconsin, Bill has long been one of the most admired figures in the Native American music arena. His album "Ghost Dance" brought him Artist and Album of the Year at the 2000 Native American Music Awards. As talented a painter as he is a songwriter, Bill dug deep within his music and his art to create a spiritual memorial to the massacre at Wounded Knee. With the words to "Ghost Dance" written on the horse beside the portrait of a warrior who fought the White Man but is able to overcome bitterness with faith in a better tomorrow, Bill has created a powerful and original artwork.

Artist: Bill Miller
Sponsor: The El Centro Mall

Fantastic Fillies

When she was invited to paint a Pony that honored the racehorse, Janee, a children's book illustrator, imagined four fast fillies charging down the homestretch, the winner crossing the finish line a nose ahead of the others. The artistry in her design is heightened by the contrasting colors of the horses and the silks of the jockeys set against a midnight-black background, and the determination and courage etched on the faces of the fillies.

Artist: Janee Hughes
Sponsor: Sunland Park Racetrack and Casino

Apple-oosa

Writes the artist, "This Pony has a patriotic theme without the usual red, white and blue, stars-and-stripes motif. What is more American than the apple? Hot dogs, baseball and APPLE pie... I rest my case." Working primarily in watercolors and colored pencils, Penny has won a variety of national awards for her still-life paintings - thus the exquisite realism of the apples adorning her Pony's flanks.

Artist: Penny Thomas Simpson
Sponsor: Eagle Ranch Pistachio Grove

Floral Pony

Known as a realistic impressionist, this celebrated Mexican artist whose paintings have been exhibited internationally "wanted to deliver the ambiance of the lush vegetation, the bougainvilleas and flowers of the semi-tropical region of southeast Mexico. There you can pick flowers and enjoy plentiful vegetation the year round. The people call their land, 'Eternal Spring.'"

Artist: Noel Espinoza
Sponsor: None

Love As Strong As A Horse

"It was a Cherokee tradition for each family to make and hang a mask in the house for power and protection, to keep in good luck and keep out the bad," says Cherokee artist Jesse Hummingbird, whose paintings of brightly colored, geometric faces have become his signature. "The two couples represent different seasons of life - spring and fall - and are my way of inspiring people to find soulmates with whom they can discover both the strength and beauty of love."

Artist: Jesse Hummingbird
Sponsor: None

Heavenly Pony

Born in Parral, Chihuahua, Mexico, Noel has devoted his efforts as an artist to sharing a vision of Mexico as a place "as colorful and vivid as a memory." Of his inspiration for his Pony he writes, "The nobility and spirit of the Horse is so high and sublime, it led me to take them to heavenly heights in the shape of billowing clouds."

Artist: Noel Espinoza
Sponsor: None

Grandfather's Journey

As a young boy growing up on the Hopi mesas of Northern Arizona, Buddy would accompany his grandfather, a Hopi war chief, as he made his rounds on the back of a donkey checking on the corn fields and herding sheep. Years later, when he developed into a multi-talented artist collected by enthusiasts from around the world, Buddy would credit his grandfather's gift for storytelling with the imagery - Kachina figures, corn maidens, lightning storms - that found its way into his cottonwood carvings, his mystical oil paintings, and his fabulous Painted Pony.

Artist: Buddy Tubinaghtewa (Hopi)
Sponsor: The Trail of Painted Ponies

Earth, Wind and Fire

Read this Cherokee artist's resume and you will understand why he is listed in Who's Who in American Art. A Vietnam veteran whose personal philosophy is "Everything is an experiment. That goes for life, for art and for painting a Pony," Bill adorned one side of his Pony with a portrait of a Plains Indian warrior, and the other with a serene Pueblo scene. Asked for his inspiration, he wrote, "From the Great Spirit and Mother Earth, All things are made."

Artist: Bill Rabbit
Sponsor: Oasis Gift Show

Wilderness Roundup

The challenge of creating a wonderful work of art on a large scale, and not allowing her disability to limit her imagination, motivated Mary - wheelchair-bound after suffering a spinal injury during a gymnastics event at age 17 - to paint a Pony. Hoping to communicate the "inner connection we share with all living creatures," she rounded up "a dazzling menagerie" of animals "in a changing seasonal environment." Over a year in the making, Mary's Painted Pony is an extraordinary achievement that carries this message: "Enjoy her beauty, follow your dreams, and believe in yourself."

Artist: Mitzie Bower
Sponsor: Tim and Mitzie Bower

Thunderbird Suite

Award-winning artist Joel Nakamura is known for his unique style - a blend of folk art and sophisticated iconography - and for his ability to convey stories in an intricate and engaging manner. Joel chose the Thunderbird myth for his Pony because "It was said that a young warrior who was both brave and fast enough to ride his horse under the Thunderbird's great shadow would gain sacred spiritual powers." Joel's paintings have illustrated articles in publications as diverse as Time and Playboy, and his illustrations were featured in the opening and closing programs of the 2002 Winter Olympics.

Artist: Joel Nakamura
Sponsor: Santa Fe Youth Symphony

Medicine Horse

Recognized by Southwest Art magazine as one of the top 30 artists featured in their 30 years of publication, Santa Fe sculptor Star Liana York is as well known for her detailed and sensitive renderings of Native Peoples as for her gift for capturing the spirit of the horse in three-dimension. With Medicine Horse, she has combined her love and knowledge of people with special relationships to animals by creating a Plains Indian ceremonial horse dressed with a collection of personal objects believed to give the horse's owner power: shields, a lance, a bow, a pipe and assorted amulets and talismans.

Artist: Star Liana York
Sponsor: E.Stephen and Kim Charlton Benson

Golden Girl

In a serene and majestic setting among heavenly clouds, the angelic Golden Girl watches the hustle and bustle of life below... and wishes for peace on Earth. A designer at Westland Giftware, Joy is a published children's book illustrator and has also worked in the children's educational CD-ROM industry.

Artist: Joy Steuerwald
Sponsor: Westland Giftware

Kitty Cat's Ball

"Here is what happens when daytime-snoozing feline souls cut loose by the light of the new moon. They jig and waltz, slide a sinuous tango and pound out a mad polka," says Elizabeth, an avid horsewoman, Pony Club mom, and associate member of the American Academy of Equine Art from Huntsville, Alabama. "By day, we only see those half-smiles on snoring kitty faces as they grace our chairs and sofas, or doze in the garden beneath the lilacs. They grin from within as they recall the gavotte from the night before and shiver with delight, dreaming of the next Kitty Cat's Ball."

Artist: Elizabeth Lewis Scott
Sponsor: The Trail of Painted Ponies

Christmas Clydesdale

Imagine a Christmas sled full of laughing children being pulled down a snowy city street by a massive but reliable draft horse festively adorned with a holly wreath... and you have the inspiration for this Christmas Pony. Mike, the Art Director at Westland Giftware, has been a designer in the industry for over 25 years. Joy is a designer and Product Development Coordinator at Westland.

Artist: Mike Dowdall and Joy Steuerwald
Sponsor: Westland Giftware

Anasazi Spirit Horse

The intricate black-and-white designs found on Anasazi pottery at Chaco Canyon, which reflect the timeless character of ancient cultures, are the inspiration behind this astounding work of art. Of French and Spanish descent, Robert has also added new dimensions to the art of gourd painting, for which he is respected and collected worldwide. A versatile artist, his horizons are constantly expanding, making him one of the most exciting talents working today.

Artist: Robert Rivera
Sponsor: Private

Snowflake

Remembering Christmas eve snowfalls at her grandparent's lake cottage, watching big lazy flakes drift through the night sky and "dreaming of the pony that Santa would surely bring this year," moved this professional musician and bookstore owner from Sunnyside, Washington, to create this new Christmas classic.

Artist: Judith Fudenski
Sponsor: None

Children's Prayer Pony

In times of great distress, it seems that many Americans turn to prayer, one of the oldest and simplest forms of communication, and one of the most powerful and inspiring. In the fall of 2001, at a time when this country was changed forever, children of many faiths from across the United States were invited to share their most prized possessions - their prayers. The compassion, courage, hope and forgiveness they expressed in words and art were collected in a bestselling book - Children's Prayers for America - and are shared on this special, heartfelt Pony that is an expression of hope in its most humble form.

Artist: Youth of America
Sponsor: Pope John XXIII and Double Star Studio

Nutcracker Pony

Drawing on imagery from the 19th century Russian ballet, "The Nutcracker", Janee, a former art teacher from Salem, Oregon, has created a strikingly original and theatrical tribute to this Christmas tradition, as perfect in detail as a Faberge egg. The Nutcracker Pony is about magic and music and family and celebration.

Artist: Janee Hughes
Sponsor: None

THE TRAIL OF
PAINTED PONIES

Welcome to The Trail of Painted Ponies, Where Imaginations Run Wild!

The Trail of Painted Ponies Collectibles and Merchandise are available through our website store and from fine retailers across the country and around the world.

Please visit www.trailofpaintedponies.com for all of the latest and greatest designs, updates and information.

Happy Trails!

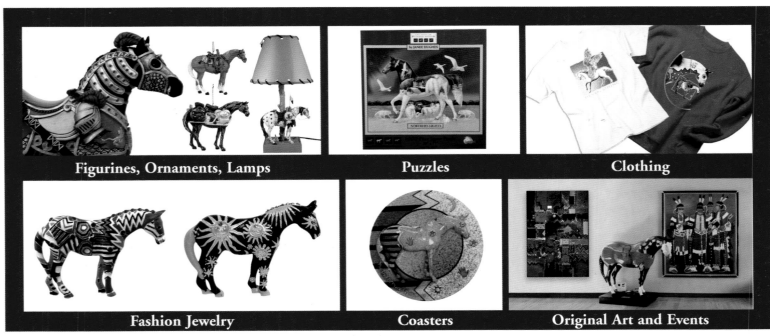

Figurines, Ornaments, Lamps

Puzzles

Clothing

Fashion Jewelry

Coasters

Original Art and Events

Wholesale Directory

Westland Giftware
Figurines, Ornaments, Lamps,
Picture Frames
1 888 888-8750

SunsOut
Puzzles
1 800 400-8953

Stirrups Clothing Company
Clothing, Hats, Tees, Bags
1 800 477-3385

Pacific Silver
Fashion Jewelry
1 800 548-8552

THIRSTYSTONE
Natural Stone Coasters
1 800 829-6888

The Trail of Painted Poines
Original Art and Events
1 480 459-5700

ARTISTS *directory*